CHILDREN OF THE STATE

STOLEN FOR PROFIT

Peter van de Voorde

Children of the State: Stolen for Profit

Copyright Peter van de Voorde 2018
All Rights Reserved
Published by A Sense of Place Publishing 2018
ISBN: 978-0-6482933-0-9

No parts of this publication may be reproduced, stored in a retrieval system, or transmitted in any form or by any means, electronic, mechanical, photocopying, recording, or otherwise, without the prior written permission of the copyright owner.

This book is sold subject to the condition that it shall not, by way of trade or otherwise, be lent, resold, hired out, or otherwise circulated without the publisher's prior consent in any form of binding or cover other than that in which it is published and without a similar condition including this condition being imposed on subsequent purchases. Under no circumstances may any part of this book be preoccupied for resale.

Cover Design by Jessica Bell
Interior Design by Amie McCracken
Edited by Bevan Powrie

 A catalogue record for this book is available from the National Library of Australia

Table of Contents

Preface 9
One How It All Began 17
Two The Criterion 33
Three Protective Contact 53
Four A Major Breakthrough: 73
Five Child Abuse or Cruelty to Animals? 89
Six The Social Costs 113
Seven The Economic Costs..129
Eight The Root Cause and Integrated Networks 153
Nine The Domestic Violence Phenomena 183
Ten The Radicalisation of Our Children........................207
Eleven Parens Patriae – The Missing Link....................223
Twelve Child Protection Reform Proposal A Time for Change 239
Thirteen Conclusion: The Challenge 249
Acknowledgements..261
About the Author 265

State of the Nation

2018 Family and Child-Protection Scorecard

- On any given day, an estimated 830,000 Australian children are deprived of the protection of their biological family.
- On any given day, an estimated 352,000 Australian mothers and fathers are prevented from meeting their legal obligation to protect their biological children from harm.
- On any given day, 1,000 suppression orders keep the electorate in the dark and provide legitimacy to Government cover-ups.
- Since 1975, an estimated 65,000 Australians have taken their own lives following relationship breakdown and the subsequent distressing consequences of failed child and family protection policies.
- In 2018, Australian taxpayers will unwittingly fund an estimated $53-billion-dollar industry that wages war against their fellow citizens.
- Since 1975, the supreme guardianship powers of the State have prevented more than 6 million Australian men, women and children from either providing or receiving the protection of their biological family.

* * *

Preface

THE FAILURE OF child and family protection policies, compounded across decades, has spread the impact of dysfunctional policies into every home.

Despite far-reaching consequences, that child protection has not gained traction in the public debate comes down to one thing: We have failed to imagine what it would be like if it happened to us.

Every child is at risk today because of our collective indifference. Consent is covertly manufactured, allowing unsuspecting families to lose control over their own children. This is not a race, gender, colour, political, secular or religious issue. It belongs to no particular group, yet reaches deep into every community. No one escapes.

Children of the State articulates an investigative journey that coincided with the 40th anniversary of the introduction of contemporary global family and child protection laws and practices. What we discovered will shock even the most hardened child-removal sceptics among us.

We attempt to throw light on why governments have failed to prevent the large-scale removal of children from the protection of their biological families, and why these practices continue to this day.

This book draws attention to the state's supreme power of authority over the nation's children, and how this power has been used to create an industry engaged in the contemporary redistribution of stolen children for profit.

Children left in the care of maladjusted guardians to fend for themselves, many of whom experience years of emotional and physical abuse at the hands of their legal protectors, have no respect for the authorities who created their nightmare and ignored their safety. In many cases radicalised and induced to hate their own biological family, they have no qualms about turning such hatred against those who caused their pain. They feel most directly the exposure to defective policies and practices. Our jails are full.

The horror stories are everywhere and could fill many books. This book attempts to articulate the root cause and provide a foundation for change.

The world is born anew every day. In a sense, the degraded level of discourse on child protection and family policies and the rapid reversion to propaganda and ideology by defensive institutions is why this book was born.

Relegated to the too-hard basket by policymakers, for politicians, child protection is a zero-sum game.

News stories are invariably bad.

Many activists are driven into the debate from personal experience, and the small band of supporters who created the Family Briefing[1] site developed an intellectual curiosity, driven in part by outrage. How could this happen?

---

1 See http://www.familybriefing.com/

Restrictive freedom of information laws and suppression orders prevent journalists from covering family and children's courts in the way they would in other jurisdictions. Ostensibly to protect the privacy of children, this secrecy conceals the extent of government complicity in the destructive conduct and consequences of unprincipled court decisions and child protection malpractices.

Here is a preview from Family Briefing on the social and economic costs:

> Every 48 hours, an additional 820 Australians will lose the protection of their family, while nine will end their life and hundreds more will commence their journey into drug and alcohol addiction or succumb to an induced mental health disorder, crippled by the utter despair at being disempowered and dispossessed of their families by the state; the annual cost to taxpayers – *$53 billion dollars![2]

That traditional media are reluctant to raise these issues for fear of legal challenges should be of great concern to us all. *Children of the State* reflects the right of the public to know, that the 40-year total of the estimated casualties for every 48 hours as revealed above, has accumulated to now having a direct impact on more than 25 per cent of the civilian population.

At the same time, the unsuspecting taxpayers of most countries are paying more for their own maltreatment than they spend on their entire annual defence budgets. In other words, we spend more on waging war against ourselves than we spend on defence against external threats.

---

[2] Family Briefing, Children of the State: Stolen for Profit, 2018 (*Australian dollars)

The police state powers that governments use to remove children from the protection of their biological families and the legislation designed to protect institutions from journalistic scrutiny make it almost impossible for whistle-blowers to come forward.

A forcibly abandoned generation has been created on our watch, for which we cannot deny responsibility. When in the years to come its victims begin to speak out, the reason for our hard-heartedness and lack of empathy is sure to be questioned.

Official government statistics demonstrate that 80 per cent of the children of separated parents are cut off from the protection of important biological family members, including mothers, fathers and grandparents.

Who then encourages, supports or defends a legal system that can only manage a 20 per cent success rate for those it is supposed to protect? Conversely, who are the main beneficiaries of a legal system that presides over a combined 80 per cent failure rate for the children it claims to protect?

Child protection is an industry. Professor Stephen Baskerville wrote in his book *Taken into Custody* of the massive and largely hidden governmental and quasi-governmental machine consisting of judges, lawyers, psychologists and psychiatrists, social workers, child protection services, child support enforcement agents, mediators and counsellors …, plus an extensive host of economic interests, such as divorce planners, forensic accountants, real estate appraisers and others.

> These officials and professionals invariably profess to be motivated by concern for the "best interest" of other people's children. Yet their services are activated only with

the dissolution of families and the removal of parents. Whatever pieties they may proclaim therefore, the hard reality is that they have a concrete interest in encouraging family break-up.[3]

Today the legal net is cast ever wider. Powerful new institutions and agencies, including the burgeoning domestic violence sector and child-hungry adoption and foster-care agencies, have gained in power and influence. Each comes complete with their own entourage of professional elites, whose livelihood depends on a steady stream of vulnerable children.

Nothing strikes deeper into the human heart than the loss of a biological child; embedded within our DNA is an inherent motivation to protect our offspring from harm at all cost.

It is not unreasonable therefore to assume that, first and foremost, every minor child would have an inherent, presumptive legal right from birth to be protected by those closest to them biologically, such as each of their willing, able and safe biological parents and extended families.

But nothing could be further from the reality.

A booming government funded bureaucracy now exercises complete control over lives and futures.

Any child born today, irrespective of the relationship status of their parents, faces the real prospect of ending up the target of any number of government-funded agencies and institutions. Their mission is to first create and subsequently service, "the vulnerable". In so doing,

---

[3] Baskerville, Stephen K., *Taken into Custody: The War Against Fathers, Marriage, and the Family*, Cumberland House Publishing, 2007.

they wield absolute power over many perfectly sound and caring biological parents and extended families.

As a result, the intrusive power of the state is now a threat to the health and well-being of the whole of our society. Unless these issues are resolutely resolved in a principled and timely manner, future generations will be damaged by our failure to act. Apologies will be made for our collective ignorance.

It is a fundamental question: how has the state managed to gather so much power over the lives of individuals, particularly children?

The answer, lost in the public debate, is found in the widespread global abuse of a little known, but extremely harmful 16th Century doctrine, which is used by nation states to remove millions of 21st Century children from the protection of their biological families.

Parens patriae (Latin for Parent of the Nation, or literally, parent of the fatherland), in law refers to the power of the state to intervene against an allegedly abusive or negligent parent, legal guardian or informal caretaker, and to act as the parent of any child or individual who is claimed to be in need of protection. In contemporary discourse, every time you hear the word "vulnerable" it is an excuse for the state to step in and remove children.

That in many cases the interference of the state in the private lives of individuals has disastrous outcomes is lost in the welter of history. Over the course of 400 years, nation states have progressively increased the reach of the power over children that the parens patriae doctrine provides. However, against every movement comes a backlash, and resistance is growing.

Parens patriae is now operating unfettered by any constraints related to its mythological historical origin. A purely judicial construct, state interest can apparently now be anything courts deem worth protecting. Never the less the false historical trappings continue to be invoked to infer legitimacy to the concept, even when they lack any meaningful connection to it. Against this tide, there has been a stream of resistance to this common law expansion of parens patriae authority.[4]

This book is part of that resistance.

---

[4] Thomas, Margaret S. "Parens Patriae and The States' Historic Police Power." p.797, *SMU Law Review* (Southern Methodist University), vol. 69, no. 4, ser. 4, 2016, pp. 759–810. Full text available here: scholar.smu.edu/cgi/viewcontent.cgi?article=4669&context=smulr

One

How It All Began

IN THE SUMMER OF 2007, I found myself in London recording interviews for a Sydney radio station. The specific program I was working for focussed on the malfeasance of child protection agencies and the dire consequences for parents and children. The show's personnel, while originally motivated by what was happening in our own country, became intrigued by the fate of the children of broken relationships in other parts of the world. We soon discovered that there was a universality of experience; that the consequences of misguided child protection policies were common across the Western world.

The journey had already taken me to various parts of Britain, Ireland, France and the Netherlands and I spoke to and recorded conversations with a number of leaders of groups and individuals in those countries. One such person was Joep Zander, a leading advocate for shared parenting in Holland at that time, and recorded interviews with representatives of the British Second Wives Club, as well as meeting and speaking with leaders of AMEN, an Irish support organisation concerned with the abuse of men in contemporary Irish society.

I was also made aware of an "underground railroad" operating in

France, which was similar to the underground railroad used during the days of slavery that had allowed many thousands of African American slaves to escape across the US border into Canada. That "railroad" was neither underground nor a railroad. It got its name because its activities had to be carried out in secret, using darkness or disguise, and because railway terms were used by those involved with the system to describe how it worked. Various routes were referred to as lines, stopping places were called stations, those who aided along the way were conductors and their charges were known as packages or freight. The network of routes extended through 14 Northern states to "the promised land" of Canada. Those who most actively assisted slaves to escape by way of the railroad were members of the free black community.

It took 300 years to realise how morally decadent the slave trade was.

The contemporary persecution of disempowered minorities within our own communities is strikingly similar and is again driving large groups of people to extreme lengths in order to escape.

Before I left for Europe, I spoke over the phone with a contact in France who had created a contemporary railroad network that allowed thousands of people from across the world to escape the often unintended consequences of government-supported global family and child-protection systems.

To this day these systems continue to persecute dispossessed men, women and children long after they have lost their families, children, property and savings and then threaten them with jail. With their backs to the wall and with nothing left to lose, his clients were numerous and they came from far-flung corners of the globe.

He explained to me in detail how he would advise his clients to borrow enough money to pay any outstanding debts, obtain a passport with a tourist visa for France, and that once in France they would be supplied with a new identity and provided with temporary accommodation in a caravan on a rural property, prior to commencing a new life in Europe.

I had been eagerly looking forward to meeting him and we agreed to do so in the south of France. But when I got there and contacted him, he told me that for security reasons he had been forced to move to a different location a long way from where I was and that he would meet me there if possible.

Even to have pursued that story, among the many thousands of intriguing and disturbing stories that surround this field, was an incredible experience since it revealed another of the many hidden but damaging effects of inhumane systems.

These are the stories of once loving parents who, driven to despair at the hands of their country's persecutory policies and actions, have been forced to assume a new identity and disappear. Denied their family and stripped of their possessions, they faced years of being condemned as deadbeats and victimised, often leading to jail terms, irrespective of what action they took. Choosing flight over fight, just as numerous slaves had done so many years before, they saw the only way to survive their persecution was to escape to a less hostile environment.

For me, this quest of discovery has offered multiple light-bulb moments. One of the earliest and most delightful was through an encounter with Tony Coe in London. Tony, who famously appeared with Sir Bob Geldof in British Channel 4 TV series *Geldof on Fathers*, at the time of our meeting was the president of the British Equal Parenting Council. He turned out to be one of nature's true gentlemen and presented as the perfect host. Following the interview, we had a great chat that in hindsight would prove to be the catalyst for this book.

Tony was well informed on the issues and was equally interested to find out as much as he could about the situation for separated families and children in Australia. He asked if I was aware of any legal parenting rights that parents might have to parent their own biological children. He mentioned that he and his organisation had sought this information from the British Parliament but had been ignored. In particular, he felt very strongly there was a missing link somewhere that just had yet to be unearthed, but that once found, would completely change the way we approached this sensitive subject. In the end that reference to a possible missing link proved to be the game-changer for me and started my own journey into a decade-long search to find the answers.

In the history of current "progressive" social policies there has been remarkably little statistical analysis of the consequences of family breakdown and the empowerment of the State over children's lives. You find what you fund for, and governments have no interest in exposing the negative consequences of their own institutional processes, particularly not when they relate to the holy grail of "vulnerable children".

Other reasons for this lack of analysis, including ideological bias, can be found. But, whatever the excuse, the failure to do so has proved to be very damaging to the health and well-being of families, children and the broader society. The dreadful consequences continue to weaken the cohesive fabric of the civilian population. If ever a Royal Commission was needed to uncover wrongdoing, then surely one that could expose the appalling state-supported cruelty inflicted upon the children and families of contemporary nation states would be the first to qualify.

Correct solutions only follow correctly identified problems. Sadly, the traditional media, caught in a progressive bind, remains reluctant to even consider new child protection information or to enter this ideologically charged arena. As a result, governments feel no pressure to change. Despite readily available evidence and a massive wellspring of discontent, no action is taken.

The facts we present in this book clearly illustrate how, for the past 40 years, the community and those elected to represent them, with some notable exceptions, have shown themselves to be either blissfully unaware or wilfully blind to the scale and brutal impacts of child-removal policies. The hope is, that good will eventually triumph over evil. The impact of legally sanctioned child removals, either through divorce and separation or through arbitrarily imposed child "protection" proceedings, is often referred to as "the biggest sleeper issue of our time". Yet there is no impetus for change, only paralysis and inertia.

Upon returning home from Europe, I began what would turn out to be a mammoth task to find the missing answers to a great many unanswered questions. Over time, it became clear that Government-supported child removals didn't end in 1975. Instead, they have continued under a different banner, which has provided an ongoing legitimacy to the practice and eventually allowed it to spread to the successful targeting of the whole of the civilian population.

That things have gone very badly awry was evident from the very first examination of the data. More than 80 per cent of all children whose parents separate virtually never or very rarely see their non-custodial absent parent, normally the father, ever again. Some re-establish relationships after they turn 18. Many do not, their mind permanently captured and poisoned to turn against one of their own parents. This is a vital child-protection issue, since the radicalisation of children into denying the existence of and their subsequent refusal to maintain any effective contact with their own biological parents and extended family, is the first step in the insidious process of indoctrination used by cults and other extreme antisocial organisations in their mission to control every aspect of the lives of their followers.

* * *

The first indication that the situation may not be quite as it appears was discovered in 2011, as a result of the detailed scrutiny of the Australian Bureau of Statistics (ABS) Family Characteristics Survey of 2009 -10.[5] It is fair to say that was the first light-bulb moment. It was noted how unsystematically and chaotically the number of nights per year that minor children from broken relationships spent with a natural parent living elsewhere, were grouped in a jumbled paragraph of percentages.

Please note how the ABS presented the summary of overnight stays that children spent with absent parents:

> ABS – In 2009-10, of children with a natural parent living

---

[5] ABS Family Characteristics and Transitions, Catalogue number - 4442.0, Australia, 2009 -10

elsewhere, 3% spent half their nights or more per year staying with that other parent, while 19% of children spent less than 10% of their nights per year (for example, less than 3 nights per month) staying overnight with the parent living elsewhere. Fifteen per cent of children spent between 10% and 20% of their nights (for example, between 3 and 6 nights per month) with the natural parent living elsewhere. Almost half (45%) of children with a natural parent living elsewhere, never stayed overnight with that parent.[6]

The devil is always in the detail however and, on the face of it, these percentages were innocuous enough. But I began to question how many policymakers and journalists would have bothered to find out what those percentages actually referred to in terms of how many nights each percentage point accounted for and how many children each percentage point actually represented? After all, we are talking about innocent little human beings who have names.

These are the millions of forgotten children who find themselves caught up in the troubled world of their parents through no fault of their own, are powerless to change anything themselves and are now reduced to a percentage of a percentage within a statistician's formula. I also noted that these statistics had been collected since 1982, and wondered what other important information may have gone unnoticed over the years.

Sensing that I could be onto something far bigger, a fire had been lit and for me there was now no turning back. Instead, further questions began to emerge such as, how many other countries collect such vital

---

6   Ibid.

information at a national level? How well and by whom, are these children protected from harm? I also began to question if these statistics were used by lawmakers to formulate family and child-protection policies and if so, was there a universal minimum standard benchmark against which the success or failure of any such resulting government policy was being measured? Even more importantly, if there is no such benchmark, then how on earth are the outcomes of child-protection policies measured?

And so began my journey of discovery into the murky world of global child-protection practices. From that initial simple first question and unexpected result, the floodgates began to open and would soon reveal astonishing answers. There were to be numerous more questions, many of which would lead to the revelation of important new light-bulb moments, each of which would turn out to be a crucial new link in an unbelievable chain.

Discovering new information or putting known information together to produce new insights, became a part of my daily routine and began to take up a great deal of my time, with which recent retirement had fortunately provided me. A lifetime of diverse, accumulated experiences and knowledge had prepared me for a task that required meticulous attention to detail, passion, patience and determination. I had also developed an insatiable appetite to try and understand the reprehensible, government-supported practice of forced redistribution of children for profit.

The temptation to exploit weak policies has proven too great for many. On a personal level, for some people unrestrained malice or financial gain operate as motives, while on a professional level many careers are built not on supporting families, but on destroying them. With rare exceptions, children are much safer with their biological parents. And yet, industries have been built on the exception, not the rule.

Strong family kinship bonds are the last bastion against the state, and in all too many cases the state has set out to destroy them.

In hindsight, the experience of five years producing a radio program on these issues enabled me to witness first-hand how the interconnected family and child-protection networks operate. Coming into contact with so many people damaged by government agencies allowed me to understand and empathise with the despair experienced by all those unfortunate enough to become ensnared. The experience was an eye-opener. Where once I assumed an essentially well intentioned taxpayer-funded system was doing its best under difficult circumstances, instead I came to see a government-supported system inflicting great personal pain, which knew no bounds and was engaged in damaging the lives of millions of unsuspecting participants.

In this process, I became all too aware of the trail of destruction left by these system networks, for which no one is held accountable and the horror of which can be traced all the way back to the 16th Century.

* * *

The search for information was certainly made easier with the availability of the Internet, however initially it was a lonely journey. The absence of funding made the search for equally committed and able colleagues difficult.

Eventually though, a small team was formed, with each member contributing their own particular experience and expertise for the benefit of the big-picture endeavour that was slowly taking shape. We now had a common goal. Made up of both mothers and fathers, we all shared the mutual experience of witnessing the pain and suffering that contemporary child-removal systems generate. Without that personal experience, it is almost impossible to grasp the enormity of the issue and the importance of what we were doing. We developed and launched our own web page, Familybriefing.com[7], which provided us with a public profile and allowed us to conduct interviews as part of our research.

We were fully aware that this project, if successful, was also bound to attract adverse attention from those who stood to lose their lucrative source of income, have their reputations tarnished or were too ideologically blinkered to look at things in a different way. It was therefore unanimously decided that in order to protect our families from possible harm and ensure the attention would remain focussed on the message and not on the messenger, we would endeavour to remain anonymous.

We were also well aware that we would be presenting this new information in an age in which global democracies were struggling. A number of books, such as *The Rise and Fall of (the) Elites: Application of Theoretical Sociology,* by Vilfredo Pareto, and in the Australian context, Nick Cater's *The Lucky Culture and the Rise of an Australian Ruling Class,* have documented the hijacking of democracy by professional and political elites. This new class or modern-day caste displays a great sense of entitlement and little concern for the everyday needs of the general population.

---

[7] See also footnote 1 or visit http://www.familybriefing.com/ – 2010

The threat of being silenced, ridiculed or maligned, for speaking out against political incompetence or persecution, or for drawing attention to the lack of institutional transparency and accountability therefore, is very real and particularly disconcerting.

We became greatly concerned by the wall of secrecy and silence that surrounds the publication of national facts and figures on family and child-protection policies. Instead, misleading propaganda dominates a narrow public narrative. As has occurred in other historic human and civil rights movements, the debates around child protection are tightly controlled by government and little scrutinised by an uninformed or biased commentariat. Rational discussion is stifled. The often unsophisticated voices of the affected are dismissed.

Debates are suffocated and opponents silenced by dismissing their credibility. Sanitised, politically correct language in what are in fact bigoted, stereotypic character assassinations, dominate discussion. Within the context of family and child protection, this is achieved by referring to their opponents as right-wingers, misogynists, deadbeats, narcissists or as apologists for domestic violence. The objective is to dismiss the credibility of their opponent's contribution to the debate and is reminiscent of similar now frowned upon deprecating terms once used to denigrate, dehumanise, marginalise, isolate and silence opponents in past generations, such as "coon", "nigger", "slopehead", "hymie", "towelhead", "redneck".

In today's world, anyone who dares to challenge the accuracy of any popular misconception is immediately derogatively labelled and their points of view dismissed and ridiculed. Other currently popular character assassinations used to stifle debate and silence opponents in other settings are: sceptics or deniers, homophobes, Islamophobes, sexists, xenophobes, feminazis, and misandrists.

Completely ignored within the context of family and child-protection policy debates are the estimated 20 per cent of dispossessed mothers, who are also faced with the loss of their family and whose daily struggle to deal with their personal grief is captured in the outpouring of pain and anger in support group forums. Alongside the 80 per cent of expelled fathers, these mothers too are no longer able to protect their children. Typically, they lose all respect for a government-supported child-removal system that has eliminated them from their children's lives and used their children as an economic commodity.

By successfully disposing of rational or balanced debate, politicians and their compliant supporters in the media are free to maintain the rage with a bogus narrative that currently centres around a phony focus on "equality". The resulting outcome for the victimised children and helpless families within their jurisdiction is, however, anything but equal. Supported by suppression orders, stifling freedom of information laws and provocative gender propaganda, Western governments have been able to suppress the debate we need to have, and by so doing continue to avoid scrutiny, transparency and accountability.

Innovative policies that have the potential to provide vastly improved protection for children and save billions of taxpayer dollars in the process are confronted by bureaucratic inertia, lawyers defending their own lucrative practices and professions who admit no wrong, leaving those with the power to make change disinterested.

For contemporary lawmakers, the ideal of effective child-protection policies are visionary hypotheses, impossible to achieve or negotiate.

From the beginning, our objective was not to travel down the same road as everyone else. Instead, we decided to go where no one had thought to go in search of information that may have been overlooked; to ask the questions no one else had yet asked and look and listen for even the smallest hint of the unusual, unexpected or impossible.

Albert Einstein is quoted as saying "the definition of insanity is doing something over and over again and expecting a different result". With great respect to all those who have gone before and worked so hard to raise awareness and bring about much needed change, overturning historic social injustices and rights abuses has always proven painfully slow.

No one yet has been able to present a child-protection reform proposal and submit it for universal adoption. Consequently, no country has until now been in a position to decree any such reform proposal as a fundamental principle in law. This is despite the fact that if successful such reforms could provide greatly improved protection for the millions of children within their jurisdictions.

But change will eventually come and apologies will certainly be made for our collective slumber and ignorance.

I look back now with the benefit of hindsight and realise the enormity of the task we set ourselves. Knowing how difficult it was to bring all the missing information together and present a "big-picture" overview, I can now say it was comparable to a huge tip truck pulling up outside my house and dumping several tonnes of jigsaw puzzle pieces with an attached note that said: "Sorry we don't have the picture of what these pieces collectively represent, but please find out what it is and let us know."

It is one thing to know the issues, and we certainly knew the issues well, but to bring all the pieces of the puzzle together, without knowing what the "big picture" end result looked like, would prove extremely difficult.

It must be remembered that 35 years had gone by since contemporary global family and child-protection laws were introduced. And these laws had allowed the unprecedented development of a multi-billion-dollar global child-removal industry reliant on a complicated network of enabling professionals, institutions, charities and NGOs.

Each bit of information we looked at, every new line of enquiry, every link we followed, each story we listened to, every new study we read, every pertinent news report we filed, each outrageous judicial statement we came across, every misguided comment made by an uninformed lawmaker or social commentator, we recorded.

While each was a relevant, small piece of the puzzle, on their own they failed to provide us with the perspective we were keen to discover. But the hunt continued, week after frustrating week, month after month, year after year we searched, listened, read and filed the information away. We were in this for the long haul, and quitting would never be part of what or who we were.

Millions of families whose rights are being grossly abused by powerful, global, government-sponsored child-removal systems have no voice of their own. Many do not understand what has happened to them. These children and families are crying out for someone to find a way through the quagmire of rules and regulations and to relieve them from their plight.

This is not something that is only happening to a minority group in our society. This is not something that only happens to Indigenous populations or only affects fathers or mothers or grandparents. Nor is it restricted to disadvantaged socio-economic groups or immigrant families. This not only impacts black, white or coloured populations, but includes the rich and professional classes. Neither does it show any respect for religious beliefs or political affiliations.

The redistribution of stolen children for profit has now become a multibillion-dollar business and no family or child is safe from its powerful reach. Global child-removal systems of the 21st Century have evolved to the extent that they now have everyone in their sights. Legislation allows governments to intervene not just in extreme cases involving vulnerable children, but in all families. No one is exempt from being ensnared in a network of systems that allows the state to remove children from their biological families and along the way relieve distraught, dispossessed family members of their dignity, their property and their savings. The loss of loved ones is only part of the immense damage that states inflict upon their citizens.

* * *

Two

The Criterion

AS TIME WENT ON and as more and more elusive information was uncovered and methodically analysed, it became obvious to the small band of researchers at Family Briefing that contrary to popular belief, most Western countries have never stopped removing children from their biological families. We learnt that children have continued to be primarily deemed by governments as belonging to the State, and are no longer recognised as the sacred centrepiece of the biological family. Effectively this means whether in danger or not any child can be lawfully removed from their biological family with relative ease, and there is little anyone can do to stop it.

Eventually we were to discover that the legal authority over children is acquired by the lawmakers of each generation consistently redefining the children's "vulnerability" status. This is necessary in order to legitimise the removal of children from their families and they do so by applying the ill-defined "best interest" principles that are now firmly embedded within national laws. "In the best interests of the child" is one of the most abused of all legal phrases. It is no accident that family and child-protection laws are complex and ambiguous.

They are so by design. Nothing represents a more grievous breach than the removal of children from a parent's care. Laws that impact on fundamental human rights are considered crimes against humanity under international law. Selectively, not so in all jurisdictions it would appear.

In earlier times, the same power of authority that these laws provided national governments was used to legitimise dispossession and maltreatment of First-Nations people and was subsequently imposed on other vulnerable and powerless minorities. These malpractices were further fine-tuned and then globally expanded to encompass the broader community, when in the 1970s contemporary family and child-protection laws were broadly implemented.

As will be explained more fully in subsequent chapters, now, 40 years on, global child-protection practices reveal dreadful consequences for those targeted, which has accumulated into one in four of the civilian population now being denied the protection of their families. In so doing, authorities have failed to protect 80 per cent of the children from potential harm, which has become a leading cause of substantial antisocial behaviour and premature mortality and morbidity outcomes for the targeted civilian population.

And if that is not bad enough, the economic burden these laws and practices are imposing on unsuspecting communities is now costing the taxpayers of most countries more each year than they spend on the whole of their annual defence budgets.

We wondered how such abuse of the civilian population was possible in a supposedly tolerant and civilised society; especially in a society that prides itself on being well informed in an era of enlightenment.

Eventually, we came to the realisation that, in actuality, very little has been learnt from history. In their distress, those targeted share a sinister historical similarity with targeted minority groups that have been disempowered in the past.

This is how that is achieved:
- First they denigrate, marginalise and disempower those targeted
- Then they persecute and dispossess them of family and property
- Then they offer copious support to help them accept and comply
- Then they make futile attempts to undo the damage they caused

Who then might be held responsible?

"They", are the enabling State institutions and bureaucracies, who have each spawned their own agencies and pseudo-expert organisations and bodies, who in turn play host to a variety of so-called professional, academic and specialist advisers. As every government knows, you find what you fund for. They know never to hold an enquiry unless they already know the answer.

Governments are likewise well aware that many of these advisers are quite prepared to compromise their impartiality and are more than willing to provide a regular supply of misinformation and dubious statistical data, as for them it secures government funding and at the same time helps to promote their own ideological agenda. Each of the above is either directly or indirectly funded by the taxpayer, and such funding is quite often further bolstered by funds extracted from the hard-earned assets of naively trusting, unsuspecting targeted families.

Conversely however, owing to our ongoing collective silence and indifference, we cannot escape the fact that: *They* are also *We* and *We* collectively have a responsibility to do better.

Why then do we not question such an international travesty?
- Community apathy, prejudice, complacency and gullibility.
- Political pragmatism, ignorance and opportunism.
- Personal greed, power and malice.
- Media editorial priorities and court suppression orders.
- Intellectual academic and ideological fashions.

* * *

It all seems so obvious now, but hindsight is a wonderful thing. It is easy to make such observations now, especially since all that information has come to light as a result of our extensive research.

Our journey of discovery first began a long way back, with the original questioning of a set of percentages, provided in the ABS 2009-10 national family characteristics survey, which had collected information on how many nights per year Australian children living apart from one of their parents were actually spending with that absent parent.

From that single paragraph with a limited set of percentages, we were able to elucidate the following information provided by the ABS:

> ABS Family Characteristics 2009-10, compared to (2006-07)
>
> Summary of Findings
>
> There were a total 5.0 million children in Australia in 2009-10. (4.8 million in 2006-07)
> 1. The number of children aged 0 to 17, with a secondary "other" biological parent living elsewhere:
> Just over 1 million or 21% = 1,050 000 in (2009-10)
> (Just over 1 million or 22% = 1,056 000 in 2006-07)
> 2. The percentage of those children aged 0 to 17, who spent half or more nights with each of their biological parents = 3% (4% in 2006-07).
> 3. There were 441,000 secondary "other" biological parents, the vast majority 81% of who were fathers. (82% in 2006-07)
>
> | | |
> |---|---|
> | * 45% of children never stayed overnight with their secondary "other" parent. (47% in 2006-07). This includes 24% who rarely or never even saw that parent. | = 472,500 |
> | * 19% of children spent less than 10% of nights with that parent (19% in 2006-07). | = 199,500 |
> | * 15% of children spent more than 10% but less than 20% with that parent (14% in 2006-07). | = 157,500 |
> | * 3% of children spent 50% of nights with each parent (4% in 2006-07). | = 31,500 |
> | * 18% of children spent more than 20% but less than 50% with that parent (16% in 2006-07). | = 189,000 |
> | * Total number of children and the number of nights they spent with their biological, secondary "other" parent (1,056,000 in 2006-07). | = 1,050,000 |

At the time, I wondered how many policymakers and journalists might have bothered to find out what those percentages actually meant in terms of how many nights each percentage point accounted for and how many children each percentage point actually represented?

I had taken a keen interest in this data previously. In particular because, at the time, the publication of the information hardly raised a mention in the media, except for one journalist who claimed that the ABS statistics indicated that Australian fathers were obtaining increased access to their children. This was a gross simplification of the reality these figures represented.

A startling fact had been completely overlooked – The data showed that hundreds of thousands of Australian children were not receiving the potentially available protective support of their biological family members. So, I wondered how the journalist could have possibly missed the broader national implications and arrive at such a narrow evaluation.

However, it alerted me to the possibility that widespread misrepresentation of the facts underpinned and thus distorted the whole debate.

By converting the percentages into numbers of children and number of nights, a clearer picture had emerged.

What the data collected by the ABS is in fact saying is that in Australia alone, on any given day, more than 1 million minor children have an absent parent living elsewhere. More than 830,000 of those children are obviously not receiving the level of support and protection that the vast majority of the 440,000 of their absent but willing, able and fit, protective biological parents inherently would be seeking to provide.

I began to realise that unless there is credible quantitative research available that supports the claim that this phenomenon occurs voluntarily, this Australian information clearly debunks the myth regularly advanced by those engaged in global child-removal systems, that most parents co-operate and reach an amicable settlement, when it comes to sharing the contact with their children following a relationship breakdown.

This myth has been allowed to embed itself into the public psyche without any credible evidence ever having been produced anywhere in the world to support it. A fallacious public perception has been created that an overwhelming majority of parents and extended biological family members, agree en masse to voluntarily abandon their children. This deliberately misleading falsehood, peddled by enabling, profiteering institutions, continues to be accepted as fact by an unsuspecting public and their political leadership, while shamefully remaining unchallenged by the media.

In addition, since only about five per cent of child-custody cases are contested in the courts, it suggests that globally, millions of children are being removed from the meaningful support and protection of their families in the shadow of court judgments. Rampant exploitation of family and child-protection laws, which now appear to have been founded on incomplete data and deliberate misinformation, are destroying generations of protective family kinship bonds for profit. We can only hope that in the future more enlightened, civilised and better informed societies will dispense with them all together.

Generations of children have been denied the support of their families because a misinformed and complacent civilian population has continued to allow itself to be hoodwinked and bullied into remaining silent by a plethora of profiteering and ideologically driven enabling institutions.

The principle reason that makes it all possible, remains the fact that the majority of the civilian population continues to wrongly believe it could never happen to them. Most people naturally want to believe their relationships will never fail and that, even if they were to fail, their partner would never resort to inflicting harm upon them and their children.

Above all, there is this unquestioning but totally mistaken belief that in the event a relationship does fail, national governments provide society with a reliable family justice safety net.

Unfortunately for most of the parents and extended families, until it happens they fail to question what it would be like, how it would feel or what they would do, if they were to be suddenly faced with such a situation. Not unexpectedly therefore, with few exceptions, when a relationship does fail, the civilian population is totally unprepared for what they will face and by the time they realise how wrong they were to remain uninformed, it is far too late and most will pay a terrible price.

I was certainly a member of that silent majority when I was a young husband and father. I kept my head down, worked hard and minded my own business. Being absorbed in working long hours to provide for my family and raising our children, there was not much time left to spend on wondering what else might be happening in the broader community apart from what we read, heard and saw in our national media. I believed the government propaganda and media spin of the day and never questioned the removal of Indigenous children from their biological families.

I even believed the government spin that it was in the "children's best interest" to be raised by white families. I trusted and believed that it was in the best interest of babies to be removed from single mothers at birth and adopted into non-biological families. I failed to question what it would be like if it happened to me and my family. I did not hear the cries of the children who were removed or felt the pain and anguish of the families left behind. I naively believed and trusted that the government would know best. The media silence on these issues compounded my ignorance, as it did for many others.

Many have come to understand how terribly wrong it was to entrust the fate of their children to established institutions, only to see those children lost to the state in a process claimed to be in their "best interest". I now know how terribly wrong I was to trust those institutions and am deeply sorry I failed to recognise the intentional deceptions that kept me in the dark for so long and prevented me from speaking out sooner.

A small beginning without doubt, but the message of the protest song, *From Little Things Big Things Grow*, recorded by Australian artist Paul Kelly, clearly shows us that with determination and resolve, from small beginnings justice can result.

The song tells the story of dirt poor Vincent Lingiari, an Aboriginal stockman who against all the odds takes on the might of the establishment and wins the country of his ancestors back from the descendants of those who invaded and stole his country.[8] In today's world, families and children find themselves equally powerless in the face of overwhelming government powers.

The words of the last two verses of this powerful protest song, identifies closely with the continuing struggle to reverse contemporary government child-removal policies and has the potential to inspire a national protest movement against Orwellian government legislation:

> Eight years went by, eight long years of waiting
> Til one day a tall stranger appeared in the land
> And he came with lawyers and he came with great ceremony
> And through Vincent's fingers poured a handful of sand

---

8   Vincent Lingiari by Ted Egan, Indigenous Australia, ANU Bibliography 14178.

Peter van de Voorde

That was the story of Vincent Lingiari
But this is the story of something much more
How power and privilege cannot move a people
Who know where they stand and stand in the law[9]

* * *

Now older and wiser, our dedicated little team were beginning to sense there was a strong possibility that, just as had occurred in similar circumstances during other dark periods of our history, there may again be many terrible consequences of large numbers of children being denied the meaningful support and protection of their biological family. In particular, we wondered to what extent governments of all political persuasions had, essentially, doctored the evidence. That is, had they used their own agenda-driven, taxpayer-funded research and statistics to formulate important family and child-protection policies that were profoundly immoral?

We also began to wonder if there might be a universal minimum standard benchmark, against which the success or otherwise of government child-protection policies were being measured. To our amazement, we discovered that no such benchmark exists. Not in Australia or anywhere else in the world could we find a universal benchmark that national governments were morally and legally duty-bound to apply. A benchmark that would ensure every minor child receives an inherent legal right from birth, to a guaranteed, agreed minimum standard of protection from harm.

We now know that there is no common benchmark to determine whether or not global child-protection policies actually work.

---

9   Kelly, Paul, *From Little Things Big Things Grow*, May 1992

Virtually every other industry or enterprise requires a benchmark to determine whether or not actions, policies and procedures are working, but not so with child protection. Nobody knows. It is completely ad hoc and completely reliant on government funding, which in itself ensures it is driven by systems born in the ideologically charged arenas of the 1970s and which provide a very ill fit for the 21st Century.

One of the key reasons for the lack of common-sense analysis of the impacts of child protection, family and broader social policies relating to both parents and children has been the lack of such a common benchmark.

Without a benchmark, bureaucrats, politicians and apologists for the status quo can claim they are acting in "the best interests of the child" without having to provide any evidence. This has led to numerous distorting idiosyncrasies creeping into debate on social policy, allowing discussion to be hijacked by the fashionable ideologies and shibboleths of the day.

Of particular concern is that the lawmakers and those who apply the law, have no effective way of measuring the success or failure of their policies and practices. In other words, they are completely in the dark without the slightest idea of the outcome for the nation's children.

This is why the Family Briefing team considered it extremely important to establish a suitable child-protection benchmark that would provide such detail. And thus, on what should have been such a simple measure, began yet another search. But this time, instead of disappearing in another maze, this search would prove very fruitful indeed.

* * *

At first, despite extensive searches, we could not find any suitable benchmark that provided for a required minimum number of overnight contact visits with biological parents that minor children would undoubtedly benefit from and on which experts could agree – anywhere in the world.

This is despite the fact that an inherent right to at least a minimum number of overnight sleepovers would be able to provide a greatly enhanced level of security and effective protection from harm for every child from birth. Instead, we found that in Australia alone, cumulatively, more than 4 million potentially protective biological family members have been involuntarily removed from the lives of the family's children by government-supported institutions during the past 40 years.

Millions of willing, able and fit biological family members have been replaced by an army of social workers and out-of-home carers who struggle to effectively protect the nation's children. Worse still, this untenable situation continues to be wilfully promoted by lawmakers and fashionable social-policy experts, as being "in the children's best interest". The resulting outcome for children who are alleged to be at risk of harm continues to be driven by the dominant view of those who claim expert status. They assert their often ill-informed, outmoded and authoritarian views of what is best for a nation's children. Meanwhile, powerless family members are forced to accept the loss of their children in silence or risk further deprivations.

There is widespread acknowledgement, particularly among those engaged in providing child-protection services, that the system is failing to adequately protect the children in their care. The training and ideological inculcation of the professionals providing these services needs to be carefully re-examined. Their contempt or disregard for biological parents and the child's extended family is purely ideological in nature. No amount of additional government funding, no amount of extra training, will correct this fundamental flaw at the basis of contemporary child-protection systems.

As a litany of disaster stories and inquiries can fully attest, the State, in almost all cases, is not the best parent.

What our investigative team also found is that as a consequence of ill-judged policy, governments have initiated deeply flawed legislation in our name to remove millions of allegedly at-risk children within their jurisdictions, from the protection of millions of their biological family members and allows judicial expediency to place the vast majority of those children into unprotected, often dysfunctional, single-parent households.

Cut off from family and isolated from scrutiny without any effective system of checks and balances, far too many children are left at the mercy of the sole parent, without any further government attention paid to their protection or welfare. Until an offence has taken place that is reported and acted upon, these children remain out of sight, out of mind.

It does not appear to concern our lawmakers that having eliminated millions of their potentially fit, willing and able biological family protectors from their lives, many of these children now find themselves completely alone and exposed to danger. Without a voice of their own and often with no responsible, protective biological family members left to turn to, millions of these children are forced to bear the full brunt of whatever dangers they may have to face. Often this comes from the dysfunctional or irrational behaviour of a troubled sole parent.

Many such abuse cases occur at the hands of that parent's new partner, where the biological impulse to protect one's offspring is lacking. There are many instances of good, protective step-parents. But the statistics do not lie. The new partner is often the greatest danger to the children of broken families. Without frequent contact with both sides of their extended biological families, those children are at risk.

* * *

No universally accepted benchmark definition could be found that recognises the need for an effective minimum frequency of physical contact visits with at-risk children.

Visitation guidelines for both extended family members and child-protection officers are entirely ad hoc.

The frequency of these visits are entirely dependent on the availability of government funding, qualified personnel, staffing levels and the ideological persuasion of agency's management.

Every civilised nation has a fundamental moral and legal obligation to ensure every child in their care is adequately protected from harm. But that is not what is happening.

A range of child abuses suffered by at-risk children, such as bruising, broken bones, burns, starvation and emotional deprivation can go completely unnoticed if the frequency of physical contact visits are either too few or in many cases fail to take place. This fact is ignored by legislators.

However, there is one thing the managers of the relevant agencies redistributing children for profit are acutely aware of, and that is the need to ensure that the flow of government funding remains intact.

They are also aware that if a universally accepted biological family contact visitation benchmark was to become the primary guiding principle in law, the rivers of money would dry up. If common sense was to enter the debate and the introduction of such a universally accepted benchmark were to compel national governments to return the primary legal responsibility for the protection of minor children back to the willing, able and fit biological family members from which they were forcibly removed, and away from the completely inadequate and intrusive government agencies, their industry would die a long-overdue death.

This would also free billions of taxpayer dollars and rebuild the badly broken family kinship bonds of a steadily fracturing civil society.

At this suggestion, perhaps even the silent majority in their perpetual slumber would sit up, have a stretch, scratch their head and ask: "How long have I been asleep?"

But global governments are not asleep. They know very well that without a universally accepted minimum contact visitation benchmark, there is no way to measure the efficacy of any of their family and child-protection policies. They know, or should, that their policies have removed countless numbers of children from the protection of their families and have destroyed the lives of many millions of their constituents in the process. They are very much aware that while the electorate remains asleep, they are able to avoid accountability.

But the winds of change are blowing and a widespread mistrust of politicians of all persuasions and of the type of national governments they represent, is gaining momentum. The public are coming to realise that these are the same national governments that for many decades have condoned legislation that has caused the tearing apart of generations of families and destroyed the lives of so many millions of their constituents. The lies and deceptions that have allowed this to happen are gradually being exposed.

Nelson Mandela said: "Any nation that does not care for and protect all of its children, does not deserve to be called a nation."

This quote was used in a November 2009 speech by now-Australian Prime Minister Malcolm Turnbull, when he apologised for the betrayal and abandonment of defenceless children by his political predecessors, their governments, institutions, churches and charities, after they collectively failed to uphold their moral and legal duty of care obligations to protect the thousands of British child migrants, who were forcibly removed from their families and transported into the care of Australian authorities.[10]

While there is no doubt that in due course many of the institutions engaged in the imposition of child-removal policies and practices upon the electorate will be dismantled, it is highly unlikely that the present-day ruling elite will be held accountable in our time. History demonstrates that the bleeding obvious usually takes a long time to sink in. Our main objective therefore has always been to build a solid platform of empirical evidence from which the stolen generations of

---

10 "Malcolm Turnbull Apology to Forgotten Australians." *The Weekend Australian*, 16 Nov. 2009, www.theaustralian.com.au/archive/politics/malcolm-turnbull-apology-to-forgotten-australians/news-story/56c2aa0bbe5618494d9c62eb1272c9b2?sv=a05cb4fdde6c075896ff56290e555ecb.

children of the past four or more decades, who will go on to provide the leadership of future generations, will be able to launch *their* own journey towards justice, recompense and an apology.

* * *

For many months we toiled away trying to find the information that might lead us to answers. By now we had become acutely aware that a great need existed to create an uncomplicated, easy-to-understand statute, which would unconditionally protect all children and be universally accepted as a minimum legal standard requirement for nation states to uphold. Tracing its troubled history, even from its earliest beginnings, we found that child-protection movements have struggled to find a common, fundamental, unified answer to an issue that is undoubtedly complicated. But, we began to notice that throughout its history, there is one common thread that has continued to render children vulnerable and which continues to form an important part of the legal processes legitimised within contemporary, family and child-protection legislation.

Many children removed to out-of-home care come from single-parent households.

We became increasingly conscious that a great majority of children considered at risk by government appointed authorities, institutions, agencies and their representatives, actually had a history of being involuntarily removed from at least one of their biological parents. Cast into a single-parent family by traditional family court rulings, these children are already deemed "vulnerable" under government legislation, and are therefore far easier to remove. The same contentious legislation used to create single-parent households is also used to justify the total removal of children from both biological families.

Once they are in the government system, these children subsequently have far more to fear, and run a far greater risk of harm, than what most would ever have had to fear from either of their biological parents.

There is a great amount of information available that collectively provides the history of global child-protection practices. Many of the innumerable books written, stories told and papers presented on the subject describe in sordid detail the horrendous outcomes suffered by generations of minor children who were seized using the powers of the state and distributed into the care of the state's preferred guardians. Nation states are able to achieve removal from family by first rendering a child vulnerable, and then declaring it to be in the child's "best interests" for them to be removed from the protection of the bulk of their family.

Irrespective of whether they were placed with foster families, in sole-parent families, state institutions or adoptive families, once removed from the protection of either or both of their biological parents and families, they are completely at the mercy of those entrusted with their care at the direction of state-appointed authorities.

And, while we could certainly add many contemporary horror stories to those on an overcrowded historical list of stolen generations of children, the main objective of this book is to introduce new information on contemporary stolen generations, covering the 40-year period from 1975 to 2015.

Despite the accessibility of significantly better information and data-collection technology during this period, the availability of a documented outcome and overview of child-protection policies is either suppressed or unexamined.

Despite the hundreds of millions of dollars supplied to favoured academics and research institutions, there is no clear-eyed analysis of the outcomes of present practices. Governments don't want to know what is self-evident to many critics. The system is failing those it is meant to protect.

What became obvious to us, however, is that there is little difference between early 17th Century vulnerable British children being forcibly cut off from family protection and transported to the state of Virginia in the US to serve the government agenda and boost the population of the colonies, and that of 21st Century children being forcibly cut off from family protection and removed to an address in a neighbouring suburb in order to serve the demands of a troubled revengeful parent or an overzealous bureaucrat.

The frightful consequences for children are the same. Denied the protection of important biological family members, they are at the mercy of those exploiting the legitimised practice of redistributing "vulnerable" children for profit.

Three

Protective Contact

ONE OF THE MOST important revelations in our journey of discovery came with the recognition of the ambiguous nature of the terminology used to define the required quality, purpose, and frequency of physical contact visits with vulnerable children. While accepting there is a distinct need for such visits, they continue to be variably referred to as contact visits that need to be necessary, meaningful, regular, significant, important or worthwhile. These terms to describe the importance of contact visits are so open to interpretation and abuse that they are rendered meaningless. They provide no child with any guarantee of adequate protection from violence, abuse or neglect.

It was not until the term "Protective Contact" was first suggested as an expression that could be used to describe a child-protection-benchmark setting, that the penny dropped and everything began to change. It finally allowed a different picture to emerge and would ultimately prove to be the catalyst that allowed us to redirect our search for answers in a completely new direction.

Wildly optimistic perhaps, but we hope that just as the discovery of antibiotics began by accident and transformed medicine, so will the definition and resulting safety benefits of the concept of Protective Contact visits transform global family and child-protection law and practices.

But change does not happen overnight.

When on the morning of September 3, 1928, Professor Alexander Fleming was having a clear up of his cluttered laboratory, he noticed one of a number of glass plates that had previously been coated with staphylococcus bacteria as part of research he was doing, had mould on it. The mould was in the shape of a ring and the area around the ring seemed to be free of the bacteria. He identified the mould as *Penicillium notatum* (which is now known as *P. chrysogenum*. His identification has been subsequently shown to be incorrect: the fungal species was actually the related *P. rubens*). Fleming had a lifelong interest in ways of killing off bacteria and he concluded that the bacteria on the plate around the ring had been killed off by some substance that had come from the mould. Further research on the mould found that it could kill other bacteria and that it could be given to small animals without any side effects. However, within a year, Fleming had moved on to other medical issues and it was not until 10 years later that Australian Howard Florey, Norman Heatley and Ernst Chain, working at Oxford University, isolated the bacteria-killing substance found in the mould – penicillium.

It may have been a chance observation by a keen-eyed Professor Fleming when he discovered penicillin, but 10 years later it would develop into an historic moment for humanity, a discovery responsible for saving millions of lives.

Our search was now directed to finding out if the term Protective Contact was already in use by international family and child-protection authorities and if not, if the term was perhaps used in other similar settings. To our surprise, the closest we could find was the reference to "Protective Custody" and, while in some way relevant, it actually refers to the detention and isolation of a person for their own safety, in order to protect them from possible harm inflicted by others similarly confined.

What we began to refer to as Protective Contact visits however, was to be about protecting someone from being harmed by their keepers. The creation of a universal protective contact visitation benchmark, will ensure a guaranteed minimum amount of physical contact visits take place, in order for the concerned person to be able to check on the subject's emotional and physical health and raise the alarm if or when necessary.

Since no such universal benchmark yet existed however, we realised it was of vital importance that a document be created that would stand the best chance of not only being attainable, but also be widely adopted and act as an effective and legal preventive measure against the harm of those without power. Specifically, it would need to be able to stand up to examination and be legally and practicably enforceable, particularly within the difficult and emotionally charged family and child-protection jurisdictions. In other words, while not limited to, it certainly needs to be able to be applied across all platforms that relate to the protection of children.

Importantly, it was envisioned that such a document would also provide governments with a minimum child-protection standard that would not only be mandatory but also ensure transparency and accountability, and be able to measure the success or failure of policies.

We spent countless hours meticulously scouring for child-protection service provider protocols and, where these were available, carefully examined their definition of statutory guiding principles for an effective child-protection visitation schedule.

We found that there was a great diversity of visitation schedules provided by institutions and agency service providers in order for children to be protected from harm.

The actual outcomes for far too many children, however, were disturbing and, in many cases, bordered on the criminal. In reality, many children were first being removed from one or both of their biological parents by one government institution, only to be placed under the unfettered control and custodianship of further government agencies, dysfunctional sole parents or questionable new guardians, and who as a result, ended up being exposed to substantial danger and failed by those entrusted with their care and protection.

In each case, these children were first cut off and denied the protection of a biological safety shield consisting of a number of willing, able and fit biological parents and extended family members. Available statistics clearly show that families and children are paying a terrible price for the ongoing failure of governments to meet their moral, ethical and legal duty of care obligations to effectively protect the children within their jurisdictions.

Even though hard to find, where adequate protocols and guidelines do exist there is no guarantee of the availability of the necessary funding or appropriate staffing levels needed to activate and implement the guidelines and provide the required level of protection for children. In other words, there is no guaranteed delivery of adequate child-protection services provided by any government agency – anywhere. Yet these agencies continue to wield absolute power over the lives and safety of a nation's children, even when they may be hopelessly underfunded, understaffed or underqualified, while the children's biological family members have been sidelined. A widespread lack of transparency and accountability further compounds the problem.

One of the very few agencies employing a minimum statutory child-protection visitation schedule that we could find was the Surrey Safeguarding Children Board[11] in Surrey, England.

In theory, at least the model they adopt of a minimum frequency of once every 10 days for visitation goes some way to being able to adequately protect children from harm. Bruises disappear in a matter of days. Regularity and frequency of visits ensures that prolonged abuse is far more likely to be uncovered.

It is hard to believe that, in this day and age of informed public knowledge and understanding of the horrendous consequences of historical child-protection failures, any contemporary child-protection agency service provider would even consider the following visitation schedule as being anything other than a minimum statutory requirement. We reproduce the Surrey board's guidelines in full because it is germane to our argument that a mandatory benchmark for Protective Contact visits must be set:

---

11   Visit: http://www.surreyscb.org.uk/

Guidance for undertaking visits by the lead social worker:
Definition of a statutory child-protection visit:
1. Seeing the child:
The lead social worker must see the child/ren at least every 10 working days unless a different frequency is stipulated in the child-protection plan. In addition, the lead social worker should:
See the child at home and alone at least every six weeks or at intervals specified by the child-protection conference plan;
If the child is a baby they should be seen awake at least every six weeks;
   Ensure that the child's bedroom is seen at least once between each conference;
Ensure that the child is seen with the parents (including an absent parent with whom they have contact, if relevant) on some visits to enable the relationship and interaction to be assessed. This will enable the worker to observe attachment, fear, lack of emotional response etc.
The frequency of contact with the child by the lead social worker is a minimum standard. In exceptional circumstances the child-protection conference plan, or lead social worker's line manager and the Independent Chair may decide that the required contact level should be less frequent.
If, in the exceptional circumstance, the statutory visit is to be undertaken by another member of the core group, the lead social worker must inform their line manager, and make arrangements for the professional undertaking the visit to feedback their observations from the visit to the social worker or their line manager within 24 hours.
Wherever possible it is considered good practice for the child to be seen on occasion in a different setting to see how they react in different situations and interact with different people.
A telephone call or email cannot be described as a statutory child-protection visit.
If a home visit to a child with a child-protection plan is undertaken and the child is not seen within the agreed timescales the lead social worker should discuss this with their line manager within 24 hours. This should be recorded on ICS with reasons given as to why the visit was unsuccessful.
The line manager should set a timeframe for a further visit to be undertaken within five working days either by the lead social worker or a duty worker. This visit should also be recorded on ICS, but not as a statutory child-protection visit. (This is because it will give inaccurate record in relation to ICS Info view CP Statutory Visit In Timescales Report). This situation should also be discussed in supervision and details recorded on the supervision record.
Note: If contact with the child is refused or avoided and the child remains unseen by the lead social worker, this must be viewed as a serious breach of the child-protection plan.
Immediate discussion by the lead social worker with her/his team manager may deem it appropriate to seek legal advice about statutory protective action. There must also be discussion with the core group members and with the Conference Chair about the need for an urgent Child Protection Review Conference.

> 2. Routine written records:
> The lead social worker must maintain a complete and up-to-date signed record on the child's ICS record, to include:
> - Reasons for not gaining access to the child as part of a statutory child-protection visit where this is the case and a child is not seen;
> - The time and date of every home visit, stating who was present, confirmation that the lead social worker spoke with the child (including if alone), or providing a clear reason why not;
> - Any information gained or observations made during the visit relevant to the identified risk of harm to the child;
> - Circumstances of all family members;
> - Specific information about key subjects such as meals and sleeping arrangements (the lead social worker must observe the child's bedroom every six weeks);
> - Factual reports of the child's presentation and behaviour (describing what they did, said and how they looked, avoiding non-specific labels such as 'disturbed, acting out, unkempt, unhappy' etc.);
> - Any new incidents or injuries, which must be subject to a full s47 enquiry;
> - The date, time and content of any communication which relates to the child and family (distinguishing between fact and opinion);
> - Child's views and wishes;
> - Analysis of information to assess risk; and
> - Evidence the CP plan has been used as a framework during CP visits and identifies outcomes.

On paper the Surrey guidelines go some way in providing adequate government protection for children. But it must be remembered that these are statutory guidelines to be adhered to by paid staff members, who are on the payroll of government agencies. Even if well-intentioned, in the end these individuals are no more than paid employees of the very same enabling government institutions and agencies that have been allowed to redistribute millions of biological children for profit over many decades.

While they are allowed to wield absolute power and control over the lives of the nation's children, despairing and dispossessed biological family members have no other recourse than to stand by and watch complete strangers manage the lives of their now extremely vulnerable children.

When placing the above statutory agency guidelines and their compliance regimes within the context of the real world, a very different picture presents itself. This is especially so since available data clearly shows millions of other children not otherwise on the radar of child-protection services have been placed into the care of a range of dysfunctional guardians by government institutions and bureaucracies, abandoned to survive the best way they can, without the benefit of the protection of their biological family. In other words, they are being stolen for profit and left unprotected.

* * *

Multiple-award-winning ABC TV program *Four Corners*, is widely regarded as Australia's premier television current affairs program. It has been part of the national story since August 1961, exposing scandals, triggering inquiries, firing debate and confronting taboos.

In November of 2010, it presented to the world a documentary on child-protection-authority failures in Australia. The program related in detail, two stories of children whose deaths could have been prevented.

The first story was of a seven-week-old baby boy who starved to death in 2005 despite repeated notifications to child-protection authorities that the child was not being properly fed and despite the authorities having previously removed another child from the mother because that child too had not been properly fed and was dangerously underweight. The mother was later convicted and jailed after admitting to the manslaughter of the baby boy.

The second story was of 12-year-old Deborah Melville, an Aboriginal girl who died in 2007 while in foster care after multiple notifications to child-protection case workers informing them that she was not being properly cared for. Deborah died in the most horrific, painful circumstances in the backyard of her foster home after an injury to her leg remained untreated. Her great-aunt and official carer, Denise Reynolds, was later charged with her manslaughter and acquitted.[12]

On the program, ombudsman Carolyn Richards, who at the time was investigating more than 50 cases involving children allegedly at risk, hit out at the failure of child-protection authorities. "I think it would be fair to say that in at least 80 per cent there was an inadequate response, and in 50 per cent, no response at all to what any normal person would consider was a risk-prone, terrible, neglectful and harmful situation for any child."

Speaking about the circumstances leading up to Deborah's death, Ms Richards said of the child-protection authorities:

> They didn't assess the circumstances in which she was living.
>
> They didn't properly assess the caregiver who was looking after her.
>
> They didn't visit every couple of months.
>
> They didn't see her alone.
>
> They didn't respond to reports from neighbours and when they visited her the day before she died, they didn't recognise that here was a girl in severe pain with nearly a litre of pus in her leg, she was incontinent, like, one look at her must have told them this child is not well.[13]

---

12   McDermott, Quentin. "Dangerous Territory". *Four Corners*, ABC News (Australia), 8 Nov. 2010, Accessed here: www.abc.net.au/4corners/dangerous-territory/8952738. Includes full transcript of program.

13   Ibid

The Northern Territory Children's Commissioner at the time, Dr Howard Bath was one of three authors of a report commissioned by the territory's government. Bath told *Four Corners*: "In an overwhelmed system you cut corners, and when you cut corners, you cut corners in all areas. One of those areas is in investigations, and we're talking about not actually undertaking investigations according to both the guidelines and the accepted best practice around Australia."

There has been an "overwhelming failure of child-protection systems", he said. "One of the messages from all around the country [is that] looking after children, protecting children, supporting families, is everyone's business." Bath then pointed out what we regard as the core message we repeatedly express in this book: "This is a problem shared around the country, in fact it's shared in the western world; our child-protection systems are failing."

A whistle-blower from within the territory's Department of Health and Families also spoke out on *Four Corners*, saying she and other colleagues had been frustrated by the failure of the territory's child-protection authorities to follow up and investigate notifications of children at risk.

She said: "Quite often I'd be told that it doesn't fit the criteria," and further claimed that a senior departmental officer had actually become angry with her when she reported her concerns to Children's Commissioner Bath.

Former opposition leader and child-protection spokesperson Jodeen Carney, also told *Four Corners*: "I think there have been high levels of bureaucratic and political incompetence. Indeed, I would go one step further. I would say there's been high-level negligence. It is shameful that governments just let it happen and let it happen and let it happen."

The fact that these cases are horrific examples of child-protection failures is bad enough, but to discover they are not isolated cases but the tip of a very large iceberg should be a wake-up call to all of us. And to even think that these failures might have been allowed to prevail unchallenged in order to protect those who are negligent, incompetent or indifferent, for the past 40 years, is even more worrisome and should be considered unacceptable.

Far too many at-risk children lose their lives unnecessarily because our lawmakers and their institutional cohorts insist on clinging to hopelessly outdated and impractical legislation that allows exploiters to arbitrarily remove minor children from willing, able and fit families by hiding behind the deleterious "Best Interest of Children" dogma. This should be rejected and seen for what it is: "offensive and criminally dangerous".

If anyone is interested to learn what the eventual impact of contemporary child-removal policies are likely to be on future generations, they should ask themselves how and by whom the children of the many stolen generations of indigenous populations were removed from their families, and what the generational consequences were for them, their families and ultimately their entire communities.

Our own investigations certainly reveal that there can be no doubt whatsoever as to the grave danger minor children continue to be placed in under existing failed rules of engagement, which relentlessly produce dreadful outcomes, courtesy of current state and federal government legislated policies.

* * *

It was never our intention to focus on individual cases, even if by so doing we could fill all of the pages of this book with relative ease. But we did make a few exceptions, since these horror stories continue to make the headlines with a sickening regularity, only to vanish into history, with the families and children involved never to be heard of again. When first reported in the media, there is an almost audible collective gasp of disbelief from the community, only to be followed by a media silence until the next brutal death or merciless abuse of another defenceless toddler at the hands of their legal guardian, or at the hands of thuggish guards in juvenile detention centres. Or, as South Australia's recent Child Protection Systems Royal Commission into child abuse has found, at the hands of government-appointed institutional guardians.

Many of these children are in the legal care and control of the very government child-protection agencies tasked to protect children from harm.

The sad part is that these cases are representative of an enormous group of invisible children within our communities who, behind closed doors, are struggling to survive the threatening environment they have been officially placed in, as a result of hopelessly inadequate and dangerous government policies, substandard institutions and agencies.

* * *

For further evidence of ongoing government failure to protect Australia's children, fast forward to 2016 and the occasionally visible tip of the iceberg of death and torture of another defenceless child within our communities.

Today, July 10, 2016, as I settled down to add to the account of my own journey of discovery into family and child-protection outcomes, I was stung by the latest front page news report, which showed a fresh total failure by a cohort of government agencies entrusted with the protection of vulnerable children. But for us, it simply confirmed what we had discovered and to the extent of which we were about to raise public awareness. The story illustrated how children continue to die horrible deaths because they are far too often placed into the care of dangerous, dysfunctional guardians and their partners, by failing government family and child-protection institutions, or end up there in the shadow of the law as a result of arbitrary actions taken by a troubled parent. These parents take advantage of legal precedent by a judiciary, who, in turn, continue to misapply inadequate legislation in the interest of judicial expediency.

We have included this little boy's case in order that his name is never forgotten and that his terrible ordeal at the hands of those entrusted with his protection, will help to ignite a large enough flame of disgust in all of us, and lead to stirring our conscience into raising a collective demand for change.

The Sunday Mail (Queensland) of July 10, 2016, ran the story of a 21-month-old boy who had died from horrific injuries while on the watch list of child-protection agencies. Under the headline, 'Tragic bungle' before toddler's death", the report revealed disturbing allegations that a few months before his death on June 11, Mason Jet Lee had been taken to hospital with severe injuries that suggested long-term abuse. Doctors had notified authorities but, incredibly, the child-safety investigation reportedly stalled after Mason's caseworker was transferred.

Sources familiar with the case told *The Sunday Mail*: "The Department of Child Safety investigation stalled when a caseworker was transferred from Caboolture and instructed to quickly clear her backlog."

Mason, who had suffered a violent death, had suffered other horrific injuries in his home just four months earlier and, in what seems like a tragic bungle indeed, he had been sent home by Child Safety officers when he should have been taken into care.

The Sunday Mail was told that Mason was found dead on June 11, but a medical report handed to homicide police showed the boy was admitted to hospital in March suffering a broken leg, severe nappy rash, a ruptured bowel and an anal tear indicating he may have been sexually abused. Doctors reported Mason's nappy rash was so severe that it required surgical dressings. The appalling injuries triggered a mandatory report to the Department of Child Safety from the medicos who treated him; they certainly had not shirked in their duty of care and had raised the alarm after concluding that Mason had likely been abused over a long period.

Yet incredibly, a Child Safety Intervention with Parental Agreement (IPA) was applied only days before the boy died. Police led by Detective Acting Inspector Ben Fadian said the boy had died a horrible death with visible injuries "from head to toe".

Child Safety Minister Shannon Fentiman declined an interview and would not explain why the boy was not removed from the home earlier.

The failure of the department to protect the most vulnerable was a scandal, said Ros Bates, Opposition spokeswoman for Child Safety. "Had everyone been doing their jobs this little fellow would be alive today."

She said she was appalled to learn that the boy may have been the victim of sexual abuse. She said police and ambulance officers wept outside the home after examining the injuries to the toddler's body.

As the Opposition declared, the state's child-safety system was "in crisis" and accused the Government of "falling asleep at the wheel".

While Fentiman said an additional 17 frontline child safety officers were planned for 2016-17.

Queensland Health Minister Cameron Dick weighed in by saying he had ordered a report into the actions of doctors who treated the Caboolture toddler. Dick went on to say "initial advice" suggested clinicians who treated the boy had followed correct procedure to bring the case to the attention of the Department of Child Safety.

"Let's look at all parts of the system to see what's occurred and what we can do to learn from this," Dick said. "Certainly I'll be looking at what we've done in the health system" and in typical fashion he went on: "Let's see what's occurred first, let's see what an independent review says and government will always take action where it needs to."

Fentiman joined the chorus and said that an independent expert panel would examine "every detail" of the case. "The death of Mason Lee is an absolute tragedy and, like most Queenslanders today, I am absolutely shocked and appalled by the reports that we've seen," she said. "In the event of a death of any child known to child safety, there is an independent expert panel convened to look at every aspect of the case … that process is … under way."

Bates told *The Sunday Mail* that information gleaned from a "Right to Know" search showed that Queensland was the worst performing state with another 1,000 or more vulnerable children still trapped in hostile families. "It often took three months after the alarm was raised to begin an investigation" she said. "The Queensland statutory child-protection system is in crisis with increasing numbers of children being left in abusive and neglectful homes."

She also said Child Safety was taking longer to start investigations and longer to finish them and that there was a large backlog of cases.

Lindsay Wegener, the director of Peakcare, openly declared that there were hundreds of children still at risk.

While Bryan Smith, the director of Foster Care Queensland, agreed and told *The Sunday Mail* that there were an insufficient number of foster carers for children rescued from abusive situations. He was quoted as saying: "This little boy had injuries for some time prior to his death."

* * *

These are not isolated cases or unfortunate tragedies, but are symptomatic of a brutally inadequate child-protection system that is failing Australia's children at every level and which has done so for many decades. Draconian legislation has created an industry that preys on vulnerable families and removes their children for profit, while secrecy provisions and suppression orders protect those responsible and provide a convenient smokescreen in order for them to avoid accountability and transparency.

Informed observers, however, are deeply concerned about our collective failure to protect the nation's children and have heard all the excuses many times. They believe it is high time that a major overhaul of the whole system of government imposed child-protection methods takes place, since the reported string of child-protection failures shows there is an urgent need to do what is genuinely in the best interest of children, instead of paying lip service to that idea. They also believe that to begin with, we need to do far better than to just blindly accept current child-protection policies, practices, promises and unacceptable excuses.

The news that in Mason Lee's case his biological mother, her boyfriend and another unrelated male have been charged with his murder, momentarily tells us a lot, but is now likely to be buried in the child-protection statutory concealment of facts, since it does not fit the popular public narrative in relation to the profiling of the perpetrator. To find information on the gender and biological relationship of perpetrators to their child victims is like searching for hens teeth. Suppression orders and freedom of information laws ensure such information remains closely guarded.

We wonder why it is considered in the public interest, that the community is prevented from learning of the gender and biological relationship between the perpetrators and their child victims. These are abhorrent crimes against the nation's children, so who or what exactly are these information blackouts protecting us from?

Where were the biological family members of Deborah Melville and little Mason Lee? They had biological fathers, two sets of biological grandparents and other extended family members who were unable to protect them from suffering terrifying abuse and horrible deaths. Why not? We ask in absolute abhorrence. But the worst part is that when one takes a closer look at the limited data available on the gender and biological relationship between the perpetrators of child abuse and homicide and their child victims, these scenarios are repeated with sickening regularity. Rarely are these abused children living in households with both biological parents present.

Alas, the voices of reason and common sense continue to be locked out of the debate and ignored by national and state governments and their enabling institutions. Instead, the dogmatic rhetoric and self-serving interests of child-protection ideologues are considered ahead of the welfare of children.

What the population is told time and time again by governments of all political persuasions is that there will be a new review, investigation, enquiry, study, appraisal, evaluation, assessment, examination or Royal Commission into what went wrong, and how they acknowledge the need to fix the problem once and for all. And, the first knee-jerk reaction is to promise to employ a number of extra child-protection workers in order that these abuses will never happen again. Clearly these are, at best, clumsy attempts to present the appearance of knowing what they are doing.

But, since there is considerable evidence that the obvious primary causes are rarely, if ever, considered in their analysis, which is coupled with political blindness and unwillingness to accept reality, it is feared these abuses will simply continue to occur.

The information we were uncovering left us in no doubt about the grave danger in which many children are placed as a result of the grossly inadequate child-protection policies. History demonstrates that turning a blind eye to human-rights violations, such as those currently being inflicted on our civilian populations, will come back to bite governments severely and will destroy many of the reputations of those who participated.

For us it was a no-brainer. For things to improve, important policy changes would have to be made, and at that point in time, our research indicated that in order to move forward and before we could even begin to analyse and measure the limited information available, it was crucially important that a suitable child-protection visitation benchmark would first need to be created.

By this time, we had become very much aware that such a benchmark would need to include practical measures that would allow a vastly improved Protective Contact visitation regime to be implemented. We also considered it an absolute imperative that, as a first principle, every minor child should be invested with a non-negotiable inherent birthright to the equal protection of both of their biological parents and extended families, unless those family members were not willing, able or fit to do so.

From this point onward, it became obvious to us that, in fact, it should be considered as criminally negligent for governments to deny any child within its jurisdiction the opportunity from birth to be protected by each of their biological parents and families in equal measure as a first line of defence against harm and abuse. Wisdom may take a long time to arrive, but that doesn't mean we should reject it when it does.

And so it was that after many months of searching for the necessary information that would allow us to formulate an appropriate universal child-protection visitation schedule, one that would be effective, practical, enforceable and was able to be used as a measurable benchmark to compute national census data, we produced the following document:

Protective Contact

Protective Contact is defined as the minimum amount of face-to-face physical interaction necessary to effectively safeguard against potential abuse and/or neglect being inflicted by the keepers of those held confined.

This is not to be confused with Protective Custody, since, in that instance, the isolation of someone confined protects that person from harm by others who are similarly confined. However, Protective Contact can result in Child Protective Custody.

Where one person has been awarded or has arbitrarily seized total power and control over every aspect of the life of another person, such power differential and total dominance by one over the other, renders one of them powerless and at risk of abuse. In many such settings, this leads to a form of socially radicalized bonding. In order to provide effective support and protection for the person at risk, a set of checks and balances needs to be available and capable of being implemented.

Evidence of violence, abuse, neglect and/or radicalization manifests in a number of ways, and in most instances, early detection is possible by means of regular face-to-face physical contact and independent interaction with outside support. Cuts, scratches and bruises, weight loss, burn marks, dishevelled appearance and subtle changes in demeanour, are all potential red flags for abuse, but can be easily concealed through the use of masking garments and plausible pretexts. Such behavioural changes and injuries rarely come to notice during brief and infrequent physical contact visits, especially when the keeper is present, or when contact is restricted to phone, email, Facebook, instant messaging, letters or cards. Conversely, Protective Contact visits provide the minimum level of physical contact necessary to effectively protect a confined and isolated person from harm.

Protective Contact is especially important in the event of relationship breakdown when minor children are involved. Unfortunately, current laws and practices place far too many children in the custody of a single keeper. In most cases, this leads to the total exclusion of extended biological family members, the very people who are most likely to be highly motivated to provide protection for the family's children.

Protective Contact within the context of relationship breakdown is defined as a child spending 20% or more overnight sleepovers per year with each willing, able and fit biological parent, (that is 73 or more nights per year). Practical common sense alone dictates that the minimum amount of 20% sleepover contact is necessary, for such contact to be able to provide adequate protection from potential harm inflicted by a single keeper.

Protective Contact of 20% overnight sleepovers can consist of 6 nights per month, or 4 nights per month plus half of any school holiday period. The 73 nights per year can all be taken on school-free days, and therefore can apply to all parents living up to 200-300 kilometres apart. However, any more than 20% of nights require both parents to reside within school range. Statistical information on these numbers has been collected by Australian and British government agencies for some years.

Four

A Major Breakthrough:

IT IS HARD TO believe that it has taken 400 years to even begin to provide a mechanism that has the capacity to measure outcomes and enable the civilian population to take back the protection of their biological children, and hence, compel the state to abandon its arbitrary child-removal policies.

At last, with the creation of a Protective Contact benchmark, we had a document with the potential to help change the entire focus of the debate from where it was to where it should always have been – *"the best possible protection of minor children"*. The urgency of the need to shift the focus of the debate from the tired, ideologically fuelled, government manufactured gender wars, which have done nothing but create massive conflict between separating parents, was now obvious.

While this book draws attention to the "protective" value that a mandatory minimum overnight visitation schedule offers vulnerable children, there is already a wealth of supporting scientific information available that acknowledges added important needs, values and benefits of children bonding and maintaining healthy relationships with both of their parents, throughout their formative years.[14]

For reasons we did not initially understand, the importance of the protective value of physical contact visits of biological family members with their minor children has been largely overlooked in debates on child protection. As a result, a government sponsored and legitimised child-removal industry has been allowed to expand to the point where it now endangers social cohesion. With 6 million Australians already having been denied the protection of their family, the end result is far from promising.

The extent of the redistribution of children for profit had at last become measurable and would be able to provide an important first plank in an essential platform for change. And, if there should be any doubt as to the gravity of the situation and the urgent need for a measurable child protection benchmark, the analysis of the data provided by the federal government's own data collection authority, the ABS, using the Protective Contact benchmark, provided us with significant new answers.

What the particulars collected by the ABS revealed was that, in Australia alone, on any given day, more than 1 million minor children have an absent parent living elsewhere and that more than 830,000 of those minor children are denied the protection from harm that the vast majority of their families would be willing and able to provide.

We focus on this set of Australian statistics partly because Australia is one of the few countries that collect extensive statistics on this ques-

---

14 Warshak, Richard A. "Stemming the Tide of Misinformation: International Consensus on Shared Parenting and Overnighting." Journal of the American Academy of Matrimonial Lawyers, vol. 30, no. 1, 14 Dec. 2017, pp. 177–217. Accessed here: warshak.com/blog/wp-content/uploads/2017/08/CR68-e-Stemming-the-Tide-6.7.pdf

tion, but the argument holds true wherever family and children's courts have been allowed to flourish since the 1970s.

The vast majority of the 440,000 of their absent, but potentially willing, able and fit, protective biological parents, plus a further estimated 2 million members of their extended biological families, are denied the opportunity to protect the biological children they would instinctively be seeking to protect.

Meanwhile, at the same time on any given day, 1,000 suppression orders prevent us from even talking about it.

It may at first appear an overstatement, but to our excited group, on a journey of discovery to understand what had happened not just to us but to our communities, it seemed that, for the first time, hitherto powerless civilians had found evidence with which to challenge the government's brutal and arbitrary family kinship destruction.

The weaponry to fight back had now become available to the willing.

We were no longer lost in a quagmire of competing claims, a closed-shop of academic and court officials, our concerns hidden by secrecy provisions in the law, and a media that had long ago abandoned its social responsibility to confront the powerful, challenge orthodoxies and tell the stories of ordinary men and women. This time information was not being supplied to the public by ideologically shackled institutions.

Commonly, misinformation, questionable advocacy research, judgments, beliefs, attitudes, opinions and hysterical propaganda are advanced by academics and regurgitated by a largely uninformed and unquestioning commentariat, thereby supporting the enabling establishment elites and suppressing popular dissent.

The factual evidence underpinning our own open-source investigations was actually collected and made publicly available by government agencies, which proudly display the national code of arms on their mastheads. The hypocrisy of the stated child-protection objectives, as measured against their actual policies and practices, had become embarrassingly obvious.

Using the benchmark Protective Contact as representing a child spending a minimum of 20 per cent (e.g., 73 or more nights per year) with each biological parent and extended family, and by converting percentages into numbers, the result became self-evident. Of the Australian children who had no such Protective Contact with their secondary absent "other" parent and family:

* 45% of children never stayed overnight with their secondary "other" parent. (47% in 2006-07). This includes 24% who rarely or never even saw that parent.	= 472,500
* 19% of children spent less than 10% of nights with that parent (19% in 2006-07).	= 199,500
* 15% of children spent more than 10% but less than 20% with that parent (14% in 2006-07).	= 157,500
* Total number of children who had no "protective contact" with their biological, secondary "other" parent and family. (844,800 in 2006-07).	= 829,500

Important results, but as it turns out, this was just the beginning. Much more valuable and damning information was soon to become available.

At long last, a new light had been cast over the way the state manages the protection of its children. We hoped we had set in motion an unstoppable train of events that would ultimately provide future generations with the evidence needed to prove gross negligence in the management of child protection.

The result of applying our benchmark shows that just two out of 10, or 20 per cent, of children from separated parents, continue to enjoy the protection of their secondary absent parent, as per the Protective Contact definition.

It also means eight out of 10, or 80 per cent, of Australian children from separated parents, are being denied any such protective contact with their biological, secondary absent parent and extended biological family.

Further child-protection failures were revealed. The statistics provided us with a window into the fallout for biological family members. This information told us that there were 352,000 Australian secondary absent "other" parents, who were equally being denied the opportunity to provide adequate protection for their biological children living elsewhere.

Upon further examination of the survey result, we also began to realise that there was another important family cohort that had been completely ignored. Consisting of extended family members, such as the biological grandparents, uncles, aunts, siblings, nephews, nieces and cousins, these family members were not even considered important when it came to collecting information on relationship breakdown and their protective value and potential positive impact on family and child protection outcomes.

This information should not be underestimated; since this government produced snapshot in time indicated that an estimated 1.52 million other extended biological family members were also denied the opportunity to provide adequate protection for the children of their biological families.

But it gets worse, since, while they may be factually correct, these statistics present nowhere near the full picture. Despite providing a regular wealth of information on the outcomes of children from broken relationships, both the public and their elected political representatives have remained entirely in the dark.

To be fair however, governments are not the only ones to blame for this apathy. Almost no child-protection-service provider, social justice activist, member of the judiciary, academia, law profession, health profession, media, human rights, children's rights or parent's rights activist among the field's plethora of services and professionals, appear to have taken the time to question the outcome of these surveys. Either they did not know how to frame the question, or they did not want to know the answer.

Here we have a government-commissioned taxpayer-funded survey, using world's best practice methodology, gathering extensive information that was able to provide the State with important data on child protection, and no one had yet bothered to analyse the information closely enough to see if improvements could be made.

But the problems did not end there. New sets of numbers just kept on presenting themselves, once the previously unavailable Protective Contact benchmark was applied to the available data. We couldn't believe the extent of the calculations we were able to make as a result of the application of our new benchmark, especially one that had the potential to make a major contribution in guiding future global child-protection principles.

Completely overlooked is that, due to the children and their families dropping off the radar once the children reached adulthood, the compounding impacts of these policies and practices have never been taken into account.

Due to the secretive nature and unaccountability of ideologically driven court systems and empire building bureaucracies with turf to protect, the dire consequences of this statistical oversight continue to remain hidden.

In particular, it is extremely worrying that the now known 40-year accumulated outcome, which can be shown to currently affect, in one way or another, almost 6 million citizens or 26 per cent of the Australian population, does not appear to be of interest or concern to anyone in a position of influence able to draw attention to this anathema.

What the above statistics actually indicate and successive governments have failed to comprehend is that an estimated 46,000 Australian children, and at least 104,000 of their potentially protective, biological parents and extended family members, are separated from each other each year, by these family and child-protection laws and practices. In other words, an estimated 150,000 Australian men, women and children are being removed from the protection of their families each year and have been both added and removed from the above statistics each year, for the past 40 years.

It is difficult to understand how the Australian National Family Characteristic Surveys, which have been regularly commissioned by Australian governments since 1982 and have had the ability to provide successive Australian governments with regular 18-year snapshots of key child-protection outcomes for Australia's children, have been totally ignored by those responsible for family and child-protection-policy formulation and by those applying government legislation.

With a variation of less than 1.5 per cent over the previous period, which can be attributed to the difference in ages at which children enter or leave the system, these surveys call into serious question the effectiveness of Australia's 40-year-old family and child-protection laws, and challenges Australia's ability or willingness to protect the rights and safety of the nation's children.

* * *

It is important at this point, to clarify the relevance of the 18-year snapshot we refer to in these analyses. While a number of Family Characteristics Surveys have been commissioned by Australian governments since 1982, each one of them can only ever present a glimpse of the time at which they are conducted. But, since upon turning 18 years of age the children are reclassified as adults and because, together with their biological family members, no further information is collected on their protective overnight sleepovers after that, any of the surveys can only ever measure a maximum timespan of eighteen years. And so by dividing the survey outcomes by 18, we were able to arrive at an estimated annual average. The annual numbers can then be multiplied by 40 to provide us with the estimated accumulated numbers for the 40-year period from 1975 to 2015, which is the subject of this book.

While our analysis clearly indicates that cumulatively an estimated 6 million of the Australian civilian population have now been negatively impacted as a result of contemporary family and child-protection policies, another 4 million biological family members also excluded from any national government survey have succumbed to the temptation and taken advantage of the many surreptitious legal loopholes these policies provide. These two divergent family groupings are lured into a deadly adversarial conflict, which takes place in the shadows of a family justice system. Many describe the experience as akin to entering a war zone. Family kinship bonds are destroyed and children end up as collateral damage.

On the one side are the sole primary custodial biological parents, who are allowed to manipulate and exploit a system that allows them to arbitrarily remove the children from the protection of their other biological parent and family at will. These parents are often joined by extended biological family members and new partners, who have either actively engaged in supporting these harmful practices, or who have knowingly or perhaps unwittingly, turned a blind eye to them in order to avoid upsetting their own family relationships.

On the other side are the absent non-custodial biological parents, who are totally at the mercy of the custodial parents when seeking ongoing Protective Contact with their children. At the time of the resolution of their relationship, these parents are generally completely unaware that they have no legal right to parent their own biological children, and as a result, are often cajoled into seeking valueless parenting plans and worthless court awarded contact visitation orders that are unenforceable. These dispossessed parents are also joined by their extended biological families. They share the deep emotional pain of the government-sponsored forced-separation suffered by the parents and children, since they are equally disempowered and left without any legal right to provide protection for the families' children.

The end result is a government manufactured perfect storm of human misery, created for the financial benefit of those "serving" a constant stream of unsuspecting new victims.

Peter van de Voorde

* * *

Unexpectedly, we had stumbled across information that suggested an estimated accumulated total of 10 million Australian men, women and children are daily struggling with emotional and economic consequences inflicted upon them by an uncaring state.

These were very big, scary numbers in anyone's language, but to think that they actually applied to the very communities to which we all belonged was frightening. Slowly it began to dawn on us that we were surrounded by millions of innocent children and families who, just like us, were struggling in silence; up against monolithic government powers that they were incapable of escaping. With nowhere to turn and no one who would listen, the daily wrestle with their induced emotional pain overwhelms numerous of our fellow citizens. Pushed to the brink of endurance, it caused many previously well-adjusted individuals to behave in ways that were completely out of character and produced many terrible outcomes that could have easily been prevented. One thing that had become clearly noticeable to us was that up to that point, history had taught our policymakers absolutely nothing.

* * *

There were certainly times when we wondered if what we were discovering would ever be believed, let alone acted upon. But we reassured ourselves that by accepting the validity and courage of our convictions, eventually the information would be tested. After all, facts are facts. We hoped that in the end, through perseverance, the truth would triumph.

Sometimes we questioned why it had taken so long to discover what lay behind the questionable and often hysterical propaganda provided by government spin doctors, because the deeper we dug the more we began to unearth. We wondered why, with all the resources available to them, so many who might have been able to locate and act upon the required information had failed to do so.

There are many possible explanations for such community ignorance and in a way we are all to blame for our collective apathy, but one indisputable fact remains as in the old management adage (often attributed to consultant Peter Drucker): *You can't manage what you don't measure and you can't measure what you don't know.*

From this point on, however, there can be no further excuse for inaction by those who are capable and have the authority to initiate and legislate reform. Any further delays should be condemned as a dereliction of their public duty.

Minor children do not have a voice of their own and we, as responsible adults, have a collective duty of care to do everything humanly possible to protect them from harm. Unfortunately, in all too many cases that harm is coming from their national governments.

***

Even though we realised that we had uncovered an important new way of looking at child protection, which in itself had the potential to provide a turning point in the debate, something told us we still had a long way to go. While we were energised by what we had discovered, it became evident that to be able to present the big picture, which after all was our objective, we were still looking down a long and difficult road. Being able to quantify the extent of global family and child-protection-policy failure is one thing, but a lot more information was needed to present a credible overview. A big picture view that would present to the world the extent of the problem and the details of their devastating social and economic consequences.

Still without any idea of what that big picture might look like and with no map to take us there, progress was sometimes excruciatingly slow. Often we would spend many hours looking for particular information, only to find it never existed, was no longer available or was subject to suppression orders.

It was evident that many more questions needed to be asked and the answers examined, before all the pieces were to fall into place. Questions such as: What were the economic costs to taxpayers of contemporary family and child-protection policies and practices in Australia and overseas? How did the information collected in the ABS Family Characteristics survey compare with that collected by the national data collection agencies of other comparable countries? What were the national social, physical, mental and emotional health costs, as well as economic and law-and-order costs, resulting from relationship breakdown, in Australia and other comparable countries? How much do national governments know of these taxpayer-funded social and economic costs? Who is ultimately responsible for the protection and welfare of a family's children? How and by whom are children removed from their families under existing legislation? Who were the main beneficiaries of contemporary policies and practices? What would need to change in order to provide the minor children of future generations with adequate protection from harm?

More answers would be needed, however, if a successful game-changing overview was to be produced.

Since the information obtained had only been relevant to Australia, we felt it was time to find out what was happening in other Western countries.

It was always going to be necessary to be able to measure our findings against what was happening in the rest of the world.

A request for information on the number of protective overnight stays children annually spend with their absent non-custodial parent was sent to the national census offices of the US, Canada, UK and Belgium.

The answers were almost identical and confirmed our worst fears that governments were flying blind when dealing with relationship breakdown and child protection issues. It did however serve to open up a Pandora's Box.

It would appear that after 40 years of large-scale government-supported removal of children from their biological families, governments have no idea what actually happens to those children once removed from the protection of important biological family members or how well and by whom those children are subsequently protected.

The following answers we received from national data agencies, show that authorities have absolutely no idea how much Protective Contact children maintain with their absent parents and extended families.

- Canada:
  "Statistics Canada does not collect or disseminate this data."
- UK:
  "The Office for National Statistics (ONS) does not produce data on contact visits."

- Belgium:

    "Unfortunately we do not have this kind of information."

- US:

    "The census bureau does not collect this information."

How can any government claim to be acting responsibly while failing to collect even the most basic data on such a significant social issue?

What is of particular interest is the fact that the ABS has been collecting such Family Characteristics information at a national level since 1982.

This in fact makes the ABS an important world leader in the collection of such data. However, a number of major questions immediately arise as to the willingness or ability of the Australian government to analyse its own data for the benefit of its constituents.

What is also of interest is the incorrect answer provided by the UK's ONS to our email request for statistics on UK sleepover numbers, since we have subsequently discovered such data was previously collected and published by them in 2010.

Possibly the failure to continue collecting this data has something to do with the fact that the "Sleepover" statistics for the UK as per the ONS[15] reveal an even worse trend – that only 18 per cent of children spend 14 per cent or more overnight stays per year with their secondary "other" parent – that they may prefer to keep from the public. Especially since this is well below the 20 per cent Protective Contact required to prevent abuse. As revealed, other English-speaking countries we approached, such as Canada and the US, do not even collect this all important data.

---

15   Population Trends No. 140, ONS, Summer 2010 edition.

However, using the Australian and UK statistics as a guide for modelling global outcomes, and considering there is nothing to indicate the Canadian and American outcomes would be any better, the cumulative effect is an estimated figure of 112 million of the civilian population of those four English speaking countries alone having been removed from the protection and care of their biological loved ones. The result of their respective family and child protection laws and practices of the past 40 years, all in the name of the well-being of families, and a massive multibillion-dollar divorce industry.

What is even more disturbing is the fact that the English-speaking world is not alone when it comes to removing children from its families, and even a cursory search as to how other countries resolve this issue reveals a global similarity so extensive as to send shivers up the spine.

All of the above results reveal crippling social fallout from deep-rooted global policy failures. If we genuinely consider the above outcomes as actually being in the best interests of children, then perhaps we need to urgently take a close look at its definition.

The use of the "Best Interest of the Child" criterion is how the people of a nation are held hostage by laws deceptively created in their name and purported to be for their own good, but which in effect serve to legitimise and empower the establishment elite to remove a nation's children from its people.

The sheer scale of the number of children denied the protection of their biological family worldwide, points to a culture of systemic exploitation of existing child-protection policies, which in turn is leading to systemic cover-up of abuse and neglect, the end result of which, is systemic denial by those responsible.

There is now sufficient evidence to show that forcibly replacing millions of dedicated, potentially protective biological family members with thousands of taxpayer-funded civil servants and trusting them to place a nation's children into the most protective environment possible is not such a good idea.

Five

Child Abuse or Cruelty to Animals?

FAMILY BRIEFING members reached a point at which we thought it would be a good idea to put the analysis of our research to the test and measure public reaction to what we had discovered. We hoped the feedback would help to steer our future research in the right direction. The decision was made to produce a media release that would draw public attention to the sheer scale and plight of Australian children removed from their families as a result of broken relationships. This information was sourced from the ABS Family Characteristics survey (2009-10).

The intention was to shine a light on something we believed most people would find unacceptable. In so doing, we wanted to expose the Australian government's failure to meet its duty-of-care obligations to adequately protect children and their all-important family kinship bonds. By pure coincidence, our endeavour occurred at the same time as the then Australian government's shutdown of the live-cattle-export trade in reaction to the alleged cruel treatment of exported Australian livestock. Our media release was emailed to each of the elected federal parliamentarians in the House and the Senate in Canberra and to a number of family advocacy groups and service providers, as well as leading Australian television, radio and print media outlets.

Titled *Why are Cows More Important than Children?*, it read in part:

> On 30th May 2011, the community, media and Government were outraged, when confronted by the cruelty inflicted on Australian cattle in Indonesia, and it brought immediate Government action. Within days a whole industry was closed down and a valuable export trade was stopped in its tracks.
>
> Three days earlier on the 27th May 2011, the Government released the ABS Family Characteristics Survey 2009-10, which indicates that since 1975 almost 24 per cent of Australians have been denied meaningful contact with their biological families, as a result of deep-rooted Family Law policy failure. Yet now one month later, we have still not seen one word in the press and there is not a sign of any community, media or Government outrage.
>
> Instead, a deafening silence greets the news of crippling emotional cruelty being inflicted on Australian children and their powerless families. It would appear the health and well-being of the nation's cows is much more important than the health and well-being of the nation's children and families. [16]

Attached was the outcome of our own examination of the ABS document which showed eight out of 10 Australian children with a biological parent living elsewhere were no longer receiving the vitally

---

16 Dads on the Air, "Why are Cows More Important than Children?", *Family Law Web Guide*, 29 June 2011

important protection of those absent parents. As a consequence they were being denied the protection of many extended biological members of their family.

With the exception of the positive acknowledgment from a *Herald Sun* journalist in Melbourne and from a handful of shared parenting advocates, there was complete silence. Not one of our popularly elected politicians or anyone connected with the traditional media showed any concern or interest in the documented failure to protect the nation's children from harm. The release has appeared on a few Internet blogs since then, but overall the result was underwhelming. It was simply placed in the "too hard" basket; where so many other heroic efforts to expose this personal torment and government malfeasance had been dumped.

So there it was, disappointing maybe but by now not unexpected. What it did expose, however, was the fact that in western democracies, the welfare of animals now wins a much higher score on the charts of opportunism used by self-interest fixated, popular-sentiment-driven politicians, than the welfare of the nations' children. It also reveals the extent to which society has allowed the dehumanising of its families and accepted its children being used as a commodity to generate jobs and justify government funding.

It is a strange new world where animals and their treatment are elevated to the status of humans and vice versa. For us this was also the first inkling we had of the difficulties we were soon to encounter in drawing public attention to a major 21st Century social catastrophe unfolding on our watch.

We began to wonder if we were witnessing the demise of democracy itself, for the people's clear concerns were being so obviously ignored.

There is an increasing and well placed public mistrust of politicians, journalists, institutions and the professions. A once respected news media has been reduced to a motley collection of one-eyed political commentary, spiced with celebrity gossip. On any given day, the public is presented with an assortment of divisive identity politics promulgating radical race, gender, religious or political ideologies, while the voices of balance and reason are rarely heard.

We witness countless journalists losing their jobs, because editorial priorities are daily converting mindless molehills of gossip, trivia and radicalism into mountains of hyperventilated pseudo-intellectual debates, while dismissing mountains of community discontent and institutional wrongdoing as molehills of triviality.

As observed in the most recent Australian federal election, investigative journalism was reduced to providing blanket media coverage of a political debate consisting of two sets of slogans offered by the two major political parties. The agenda was set not by the media but by those running for public office and the narrow choice offered the electorate was to accept either the "Privatisation of Medicare" or the "Jobs and Growth" mantra as gospel. Nothing in the campaigns reflected the lived experience of constituents.

One was a devious thought bubble fabricated by the daughter of a former Federal treasurer, while the other was a mind numbingly ambiguous term created by a brain-dead creative genius in the office of the Prime Minister.

Serious debate on the failure by our elected representatives to provide adequate protection for Australia's children and their families continues to be non-existent and media interest, miniscule. None of the readily available statistics are ever considered worthy of scrutiny.

Credible evidence and the facts simply do not fit the government narrative and is a "hard sell" for media executives.

Such widespread disinterest has allowed the expansion of extensive interconnected child-redistribution networks to go unchallenged. Consisting of an integrated collection of public and private institutions and agencies, these networks have greatly expanded their sphere of influence and now, on the rare occasion these issues enter the public discourse, dominate.

No alternative voices are heard.

If there should be any doubt about the shared historic similarity of consequences suffered by the children of today as a result of government policies, the Australian Institute of Family Studies' explanation in its *History of Child-Protection Services*, is well worth considering. It refers to the sad case of 10-year-old American girl Mary Ellen McCormack, whose abusive, adoptive mother was charged in New York under the cruelty to animals act in the 1870s. In the subsequent court case, Mary Ellen was referred to as a "human animal" and therefore seen as entitled to protection comparable to that given to animals.

> The first manifestations of child protection services with a legal mandate to intervene to protect children from abuse and neglect emerged in the late 19th Century, initially in the form of charitable and philanthropic endeavours (Jeffreys & Stevenson, 1996). Often referred to as the first wave of the child rescue movement, developments in the United States and the United Kingdom helped to pave the way for change in Australia. In the United States, the much-publicised case of Mary Ellen McCormack in the 1870s is widely accepted

as the catalyst for the creation of laws to protect children from maltreatment by caregivers. Mary Ellen McCormack was a 10-year-old girl who experienced ongoing physical abuse by her adoptive mother in New York. As there were no laws to protect children from cruelty, the American Society for the Prevention of Cruelty to Animals was approached to assist. It took the case to court on the basis that Mary Ellen was a "human animal" and therefore entitled to protection comparable to that given to animals. The case saw Mary Ellen placed in an orphanage and her caregiver imprisoned.[17]

So how far have we really come? How well are our children really protected in the 21st Century compared to the protection offered animals?

If the aforementioned recent case of the brutal murder of Mason Jet Lee and the failure of child-protection services to prevent his death tells us anything, it is that, shamefully, we have learned absolutely nothing.

Knee-jerk reactions to perceived animal cruelty continue to take centre stage. But deaths, abuse and neglect of minor children by dysfunctional caregivers appointed by national government agencies does not rate any decisive action. Much hand-wringing and shedding of crocodile tears, along with further rounds of futile promises and more time-wasting reviews of their policies and practices, have achieved nothing. In the demoralised state into which our democracies have slipped, not even a Royal Commission or parliamentary enquiry into our scandalous national child-removal and protection

---

17 Australian Institute of Family Studies, "History of Child Protection Services", *CFCA Resource Sheet* – January 2015

failures would solve the problem. These inquiries are notoriously useless, a bonanza for lawyers and a face-saving device for politicians. Their recommendations are rarely implemented.

There is a growing realisation that compared to abused animals, the sickening treatment of abused children at the hands of dysfunctional carers will continue to barely pique the interest of our political leadership. With ideologues running rampant in the arena, common sense has gone out the window. For a politician, it is easier to turn a blind eye. For bureaucracies, keen to avoid waves of litigation from damaged individuals, it is easier to persist with the lie that they did indeed act "in the best interests of the child".

Every time a child is severely abused or killed in horrific circumstances, or simply goes missing without a trace, the public is bombarded with a flurry of empty rhetoric manufactured by those responsible for systemic policy failure, and merely serves to dull the senses of an outraged public following the unnecessary death or torture of another defenceless child.

Time and time again, the heroic promises made by our elected officials to improve the grossly ineffectual, interconnected systems responsible for the protection of children, has proven to be hollow nonsense. The denial of responsibility is deceptive propaganda provided by institutional heavyweights desperate to protect their reputations and government funding, rather than urgently address needed policy changes founded on empirical evidence.

* * *

Fast forward another five years to 2016 - 2018, during the period of writing this book, and once again, the knee-jerk government reaction to alleged animal cruelty is evidenced.

In 2016, the New South Wales state government introduced a greyhound racing ban, professing great concern for the welfare of the animals. While at the same time, they chose to remain silent on the welfare of children. Two years later in 2018, we again witnessed government animal cruelty concerns, with regard to the mistreatment of sheep that exposed deplorable conditions during live export journeys on vessels. This time we observed an outraged Federal Agriculture Minister threatening to jail company directors in a bid to improve animal welfare across the industry.[18] While the Federal Opposition called for a complete ban on the industry.[19]

Once again it illustrated sickening hypocrisy. One could not help feeling that perhaps the prevention of horrific acts of cruelty to children would be far better off being adjudicated within the jurisdiction of the Prevention of Cruelty to Animals Act, instead of persisting with the current lamentable, ineffectual child-protection legislation.

Inquiries around the country consistently show major problems.

Community backlash is already evident in the rising tide of public contempt for government and the institutions tasked with child protection.

With 6 million, or one quarter of the Australian population, now having been denied the protection of their biological family, the resul-

---

18 Tillett, Andrew. "Shutting Down Sheep Trade Would Have Little Economic Impact on Farmers." (Australian) *Financial Review*, 9 Apr. 2018, Sydney. Accessed here: www.afr.com/news/shutting-down-sheep-trade-would-have-little-economic-impact-on-farmers-report-finds-20180409-h0yi7c

19 Worthington, Brett, ABC Rural, "Live sheep exports: Labour calls for a complete ban, wants processing to happen within Australia.", May 3, 2018

tant lack of social cohesion and extreme levels of personal disengagement will, many fear, form key underlying factors driving the violent political and social revolutions to come.

What unites the whole of an unsuspecting electorate is a shared vulnerability to their children being removed from their protection at the behest of an intimidating but shamefully legitimised child-removal industry, which in turn requires a constant stream of "vulnerable" children to maintain profit margins, preserve their influence and justify their existence.

A possible non-violent outcome could be achieved if a well organised and highly motivated alliance of minority groups could be found. Such an alliance might consist of Indigenous/First Nation people, together with a dedicated union movement concerned at such harmful social-justice policy failure and possibly joined by a major religious organisation keen to recover its moral standing. Such a grouping might conceivably produce a nationally respected leadership group willing to form a united front and recognise and denounce contemporary child-removal policies.

The leadership of such alliance would need to be prepared to condemn the predominately white silent majority for their apathy, muteness and failure to recognise the large-scale removal of the broader community's own children, as well as those being removed from our Indigenous brothers and sisters.

With creative vision, a jointly contested class action test case may well be initiated within the jurisdiction of the Prevention of Cruelty to Animals Act.

In support of such a possibility, the Australian Museum on its official website in bold letters, defines humans as members of a large group of animals known as mammals (Class Mammalia). Humans are further defined by the same museum as belonging to a particular subgroup of mammals known as the primates (Order Primates).

Such a test case would have the effect of challenging catastrophically Orwellian legislation, which is perpetuated by community apathy and is allowing the abuse of so many of the nation's children to continue.

Governments so challenged would be exposed to extensive public scrutiny and their accountability and record on responsibly caring for the safety and welfare of the nation's children severely tested. This is particularly so since only governments hold the legislative power to direct where children will live and who will protect them from harm.

The removal of children from the protection of their families in order to placate a feeding frenzy by child-hungry, government-supported institutions and agencies, is witnessed in many parts of the developed world.

In a morally decaying, hyper-vigilant and trigger-happy US, the late Georgian State Senator Nancy Schaefer, 50th District – who many claim was murdered along with her elderly husband following the release of her damning report exposing extensive corruption in child-protection services – allegedly lost her life because she dared to challenge the institution responsible for widespread state-supported child removals for profit. Police claim it was a murder-suicide and closed the case. In her highly critical report, she laments the inhumane injustices inflicted upon her fellow citizens through policies created by elected representatives:

> Having worked with probably 300 cases state-wide, and now hundreds and hundreds across this nation and in nearly every state, I am convinced there is no responsibility and no accountability in the Child Protective Services system ... On my desk are scores of cases of exhausted families and terrified children. It has been beyond me to turn my back on these suffering, crying, and beaten down individuals. We are mistreating the most innocent. Child Protective Services have become an adult centred business to the detriment of children ... I have witnessed such injustice and harm brought to so many families that I am not sure if I even believe reform of the system is possible! The system cannot be trusted. It does not serve the people. It obliterates families and children simply because it has the power to do so.[20]

The complex and sometimes unfamiliar arguments required to progress a comprehensive child-protection debate urgently need to be ventilated. The fact that we have got to a stage where everyone is too scared to raise these issues and engage in a balanced debate for fear of reprisals is reprehensible. Any issue around child protection needs to be at the forefront of our national conversation.

It is an issue of paramount importance to the whole community irrespective of gender, colour, religious beliefs or social standing. Our elected parliamentary representatives have an obligation to debate this in parliament. That is the role of good government.

If any child is being abused it is incumbent upon all decent people

---

20 Schaefer, Nancy, Senator 50th District, *The Corrupt Business of Child-Protection Services*, 16 November 2007.

to speak up. There is no justifiable reason to remain silent or ignore such abuse. Anyone who fails to say something will find that, in due course, the focus will be on them to explain why they remained silent when their sense of moral courage was challenged.

Any grandparent who suspects their biological grandchildren are possibly being abused while in the care of their own child or while in the care of their child's current or ex-partner, has a duty of care to report such suspicions to the authorities. If, as so often happens, the relevant authorities do not respond to the grandparents' fears, they in turn need to be held accountable for any abuse those children suffer.

Shamefully, while contemporary legislation abandons thousands of powerless minor children into the care of dysfunctional guardians each year, with many of them facing abusive situations completely alone because of our collective myopia, we are reassured that those abusing animals will be severely punished.

National Prevention of Cruelty to Animal Acts provide for a comprehensive protective safety shield for animals, while at the same time child protection authorities knowingly return many abused children right back into the care of known abusers due either to a lack of training and funding, or worse still, as a result of judicial, political, institutional or ideological expediency.

* * *

Family Briefing determined to research into how exactly the abuse and neglect of animals was defined in our national laws and what the penalties were for the perpetrators of such abuse and neglect. We again discovered there are no uniform international laws and a wide range of penalties are applied in the various states and territories. In Australia alone, these penalties range from a maximum one-year jail term and a fine of $13,700 in the Northern Territory, to a maximum seven-year jail term and a fine of $235,600 in the state of Queensland.

Penalties for animal cruelty offences vary in each jurisdiction, but all have provisions for jail terms and fines. The maximum penalties can apply to both deliberate and negligent acts of animal cruelty. Both state and national governments have clearly shown that they have both the willingness and capacity to shut down entire industries in order to protect animals.

When it comes to acting on reports of gross failure to protect the nation's children as opposed to the protection of animals, however, an interesting picture has emerged.

According to a report produced by the Australian Institute of Health and Welfare (AIHW), *Child Protection Australia 2014-15*, child abuse and neglect is alleged to be one of Australia's biggest and most misunderstood social problems. This document reports that 42,457 Australian children were allegedly abused or neglected in one year alone.

It goes on to say that one child every 13 minutes suffers physical, sexual, emotional abuse or neglect, often by someone they know and should be able to trust; most often in their own home. The report further claims that thousands additional cases go unreported, and that the number of children and young people in out-of-home care is increasing. Yet, there is no public outcry from the community, traditional media or our elected representatives. Why?

Our own analysis of open source information provides the unreported side of a debate we need to have. It soon became obvious that reports such as these generally tend to only tell half the story. They predominately serve to alarm the public and by so doing, justify enormous interconnected networks of taxpayer-funded public and private institutions and agencies, created by governments, to remove and service these allegedly "vulnerable" children. By so doing, they enable the destruction of despairing families and the fabric of the communities in which they live.

The AIHW report on the number of Australian children who have earlier been categorised as "vulnerable" details the kind of support and outcomes produced by a burgeoning government-funded industry that is increasingly outsourcing services to private for-profit organisations.

What is never mentioned is the fact that literally tens of thousands of unfortunate children begin their perilous journey into forced care after initially winding up in the custody of sole-carer households who have, with the full encouragement of the state and without understanding the consequences of their own actions, denied their children the protection of their extended biological families. These children begin their flight into precarious and hidden environments where they are often exposed to a range of grave dangers.

Many of these children are further endangered from the moment they are taken into the direct care of the government, where they are forced into foster care, adopted by government-approved strangers, or secreted in various institutions at the mercy of delegated guardians.

That defenceless children need protecting from harm goes without saying and is not at issue, but we certainly question the walls of silence, lack of transparency and the way crucial information is withheld from public scrutiny.

The reason why and how so many children end up in such precarious and often extremely dangerous situations is never discussed in detail. That those reasons would provide the community and legislators with a better insight into the extent and diversity of many of the underlying causal factors and so prevent many children and families from unnecessary suffering, is completely ignored. Worse still, is the readily available evidence that suggests such ignorance is widespread, deliberate and well-orchestrated.

Any parent today, who considers themselves a good parent and therefore comfortably insulated from ever having their children removed from their care and protection, is living in a fool's paradise. Such blissful ignorance is precisely what the removal industry relies upon when they need more children to sustain the constant supply required by the child-protection sector.

That so many people are allowed to profit from other people's children in what we like to think of as a civilised society defies belief. That such behaviour is legitimised and initiated by national governments may also help to explain the steady drift away from conventional political parties, by a dispossessed and disenchanted electorate.

Ideology plays an all too rampant part in the study of child abuse, which is clearly exemplified by the AIHW's handling of the issues.

While one of the government's most respected research authorities, its reputation for neutrality and high-quality analysis has been damaged by a dispute over the gender of perpetrators and the biological relationship those perpetrators have to their child victims.

The institution has received many Freedom of Information (FOI) requests relating to a long-term cover-up regarding the gender of child abuse perpetrators, data it has contentiously refused to publish. The manipulation by the organisation to deliberately conceal such important information is disturbing. It is precisely this susceptibility to pressure from ideologically driven groups, which keep the public ignorant and allow current child-removal policies to flourish.

Challenging the refusal by both national and state governments to publish details on the profiles of perpetrators of child abuse and neglect, prominent Australian psychologist and writer Bettina Arndt is contemptuous of the persistent refusal to release such important details.

> The one time this body published this data was twenty years ago in 1996 and showed 968 male to 1,138 women perpetrators. Since then, FOI requests have produced data only from Western Australia, namely state Department for Child Protection figures that show the numbers of mothers responsible for "substantiated maltreatment" between 2007 and 2008 rose from 312 to 427. In the same period the number of fathers reported for child abuse dropped from 165 to 155. It's easy to see why bureaucrats would be nervous about figures like that.[21]

The question on everyone's lips therefore is, why have these government policies and practices that are the root cause of so much unnecessary pain, stress and anger, been allowed to carve such a path of destruction through our communities for the past four decades, almost completely unchallenged?

---

21 Arndt, Bettina. "Silent Victims – Both Mothers and Fathers Can Be Violent." *The Australian*, 14 Nov. 2015.

Are we not engaged in a morally bankrupt group-think that exposes our collective lack of compassion, empathy and concern for the legitimised child abuses being inflicted on the nation's children in our name?

But the chickens will come home to roost. They always do.

Finally, in 2016, we have seen a number of Royal Commissions begin to lift the lid on a range of institutional child-abuse situations, the scale of which is unprecedented.

The recent South Australian Royal Commission into institutional child abuse, reported findings of the commission that were scathing of child-protection authorities and their failure to prevent the abuse of children placed in their care. Evidence of abuses and cover-up were also reported to have been rampant and were ignored by authorities.

The Royal Commission into institutional child abuse ordered by former Australian Prime Minister Julia Gillard has been a highly lucrative "lawyer fest", focusing on historic cases in religious institutions. Many of the alleged perpetrators have already passed away, for some their names muddied forever by hearsay evidence that can never be proved. For others, the atrocious abuse of children in their care has finally been exposed.

No doubt bad things happened for many decades in many institutions that can never ever be excused, but where were the law enforcement agencies, medical professionals, human rights commissions, politicians, traditional media and child-protection agencies, during the many decades they received frantic calls for help from the victimised children and their families?

Just like their ineffective predecessors, current national and state governments along with their taxpayer-funded institutions have neither the gumption nor the courage to expose the many abuses occurring on *their* watch. Often inflicted by perpetrators within bureaucracies tasked with the care of children, these abuses continue to balloon unimpeded, without due investigation or oversight. Many of the perpetrators operate without fear of indictment owing to the protection offered by the legal umbrella of family and children's courts.

The lid was blown off one of these contemporary abuses when again the ABC's *Four Corners* program broadcast horrific images of a scantily clad teenage boy being assaulted and later with a hood over his head, being locked into a restraining apparatus by Don Dale Youth Detention Centre staff in Northern Territory.

Prime Minister Malcolm Turnbull hastily called a Royal Commission into the abuse of children under custodial care at the centre.

At Family Briefing we had heard it all before and issued a media release:

> Another Royal Commission will do nothing but line the pockets of lawyers to tell us what we already know.
>
> The horrific abuse of teenagers in detention centres as exposed on the ABC *Four Corners* program has been known to authorities for many years.
>
> That Indigenous Affairs Minister Nigel Scullion did not initially look at the footage despite having been alerted to its impending broadcast and claimed to not have previously seen evidence sufficient to pique his interest, simply defies belief.
>
> Prime Minister Malcolm Turnbull can be as "shocked and

appalled" as he likes, but he sits atop a system of chronic child-protection mismanagement to which successive governments have been either wilfully blind or blissfully ignorant for many decades.

* * *

The past 40 years has witnessed the quiet metamorphosis of a once community friendly system of family and child protection laws, originally envisioned to serve as a well-intentioned system of public assistance, into nothing less than a miniature penal apparatus, replete with its own tribunals, prosecutors, police, and punishments. Today, we have a broken system of juvenile and family courts, awash with matrimonial lawyers, child-protective services, domestic-violence units, child-support enforcement agents, and a host of taxpayer-funded advocacy groups and service providers, all ready to share in the ill-gotten spoils of present-day child removals for profit.

From its very beginning promoted as being in "the best interests of children", most nation states have continued to phase in a host of creative changes over time, most of which serve to justify an ever-expanding industry.

In 1980, the US created an industry in which people could make a living by raising other people's children. One research analyst reported, "This was made possible with the passage of the Adoption Assistance and Child Welfare Act, which required states to pay people to adopt removed children with "Special Needs". Without specifying what those needs were, they simply defined the "Special Needs" as "children who cannot be returned to the parents' home". Child-Protection Services (CPS) were granted almost unlimited power to remove children from their families by abolishing judicial oversight and the requirement for them to go through due process.[22]

Then in 1997, US Congress passed the Adoption and Safe Families Act, which allowed the federal government to pay states for the number of children they placed in adoption. "It allows the states to terminate parental rights for children in foster care, and circumvents all of the Bill of Rights as far as Searches and Seizures, the right to Life, Liberty, and the Pursuit of Happiness, the 5th Amendment, and much more."[23]

Laws such as these are taken straight from the pages of Adolf Hitler's *Mein Kampf*. He offered the following chilling advice on what action a government should take in order to control its people:

> The state must declare the child to be the most precious treasure of the people. As long as the government is perceived as working for the benefit of the children, the people will happily endure almost any curtailment of liberty and almost any deprivation.[24]

By adopting Hitler's advice, many countries have created child-trafficking systems, which provide financial incentives for governments to remove children from their parents. The catastrophic consequences of this are that if you come within the compass of any child protection services radar anywhere in the world, you will find that neither you nor your children have any rights whatsoever. Period.

---

22 "Child Protective Services - Heroes or Villains?" Hiding the Truth, 22 Jan. 2016, Accessed here: www.hidingthetruth.com/child-protective-services-heroes-or-villains/.
23 Ibid
24 *Mein Kampf*, originally published by Houghton Mifflin of Boston, 1943.

In the US alone, a multibillion-dollar industry is now firmly entrenched, with millions of people dependent on ever increasing numbers of adoptions.

There is also considerable concern across America that child-abuse statistics may be inflated in order to keep the money flowing. Since the stakes are so high and because the CPS is immune to any auditing other than its own, even from Congress, getting actual numbers is extremely difficult.

The staggering number of children legally redistributed for profit around the world has accumulated into a global epidemic of stolen children that is leaving a trail of despairing broken families and communities in its wake.

According to statistics collected and published by many national governments, the resulting number of children ending up spending time in out- of-home care also continues to rise. A small global glimpse into an insidious growing problem can be found in the national statistics provided by the following countries:

2013	Canada	62,428 children
2015	Australia	43,400 children
2015	USA	670,000 children
2016	UK	94,000 children

Sadly this is only the tip of the iceberg, since these statistics merely represent the number of children being removed from the *whole* of their biological family. Millions more are removed by the authorities from the protection offered by *most* of their biological family members, preferring to abandon them into the sole care of a dysfunctional custodial carer, where far too often, subsequent carer behaviour has placed many of those children in danger.

"In order to conform to the welfare model of one custodial parent and one non-custodial parent, divorce-court judges who might otherwise be inclined to allow both parents a shared role in parenting their children, are pressured into judicial expediency and evict one of them," writes Professor Stephen Baskerville. "Parents who are fit, willing and able to care for their children are designated as 'absent', with the implication that they have 'abandoned' their children, when in fact they have clearly done no such thing."[25]

In Australia, the voices of discontent are also growing louder. Grandmothers Against Removals (GMAR),[26] is a network of Indigenous families directly affected by forced child removals. These brave community elders are calling for protests to continue the fight against the mass removal of children from their families by "child-protection" services enforced by the police. The end result is a growing number of adolescents shut away in juvenile prisons.

GMAR states that the recent media exposure of the torture of children in Northern Territory youth detention centres is symptomatic of the institutionalised abuse perpetrated by these systems of forced removal. The group also draws attention to the fact that the number of Aboriginal children in out-of-home care is now higher than ever and rising rapidly, claiming that far more children are being taken today than during the time of the Stolen Generations of the 20th Century. The numbers have increased 400 per cent since Australian Prime Minister Kevin Rudd's much hyped "apology" for the wrongs of the past.

---

25 Baskerville, op. cit., 2007.
26 GMAR, formed in 2014, http://stopstolengenerations.com.au/about-gmar

GMAR further assert that the proportion of children being placed with their Aboriginal families is also steadily declining, with many ending up in the juvenile detention system and that Aboriginal children are now 28 times more likely to be in prison than non-Aboriginal children.

Governments lie.

Governments prey on the vulnerable.

Governments ignore the anguish of the populace.

Governments are destroying the social fabric of the next generation.

Ignored is the damage they are doing to children, all day, every day.

The cruellest twist of all, governments protect animals better than they protect children.

Six

The Social Costs

THE TRUTH WILL OUT.

When thinking of the costs of relationship breakdown and the intertwined child-protection and removal industries, most people think immediately of the financial costs, which are covered in detail in the next chapter. But equally, if not more importantly, so are the social costs.

During the course of accumulating a mountain of crucial data, Family Briefing collected hours of audio testimonies.[27] Many of those were recordings of now-adult child victims, speaking candidly of the torment and hopelessness of the deprivations they suffered as children. Inevitably, these experiences follow the relationship breakdown of their biological parents. These are representative of the voices of millions of children denied the protection of crucial family members and who continue to be left in the primary care of questionable legal guardians. Appointed by governments, these custodians are the nominated non-biological strangers or non-compliant biological primary carers who are driven by greed, malice, power or

---

27 See http://www.familybriefing.com – *Children of the State* (MP3) Parts 1, 2, 3 and 4.

ideology. With absolute impunity, they are allowed to exploit weak family and child protection laws riddled with legal loopholes for their own personal advantage.

We now know decades of collective inertia have produced a social engineering disaster that has damaged the lives of many Australians. To our great shame we continue to ignore the fact that we are legitimising the redistribution of children for profit. We are in essence engaged in the universally discredited practice of human trafficking.

The redistribution of humans for economic gain is generally acknowledged as referring to human trafficking and is considered unacceptable by most nation states. We as a community have yet to acknowledge or even understand the extent of our collective involvement.

It should be noted however, that at no point did we ever consider the unacceptable behaviour of so many dysfunctional primary caregivers as representing the behaviour of all legal guardians. We have never questioned the fact that the vast majority of primary caregivers instinctively consider the protection of their biological children their number one priority. Many legal guardians appointed by governments, whether biological or not, are also decent and responsible adults who have a strong commitment to the welfare of the children under their care.

But, so were most of those who adopted generations of stolen Aboriginal children. We now know the damage that follows legitimised attempts at forced re-socialisation of a powerless minority population. These mostly well-meaning adoptive parents, along with government sponsored institutions, unwittingly allowed themselves to become complicit in the stealing of other peoples' children for profit.

The enormous impact removals of Aboriginal children have had on their health, well-being and human suffering is profound, is well-documented and reverberates throughout the Indigenous communities of today.

At the time, the broader community, descendants of a predominantly European migrant population, felt the issue did not really apply to them and remained blissfully ignorant of the catastrophic social consequences. We are embarrassingly slow learners.

Naïvely, we continue to blindly accept the government spin of the day, that it is in "the best interest of children" for them to be removed from their allegedly unfit biological families on the bases of the flimsiest of allegations.

While we foolishly remain convinced that this will only happen to other people's children, public interest will continue to remain minimal.

The fact that this problem has reached everyone's front porch is largely ignored, but ignorance is of no help when the knock comes on your door and it is your turn to hand over your children to the authorities on account of someone pointing a condemnatory finger at you and your family.

To our collective shame, we no longer question the validity of the allegations levelled against the parents of those children and in so doing, remain oblivious to the fact that the vast majority of those allegations are never substantiated, but simply serve to permanently remove children from their families. We have lost the ability to empathise with the utter despair and suffering experienced by countless disempowered families throughout our communities, because we foolishly do not think it could ever happen to us.

No government that treats its own citizens with such disregard, such blazing contempt, is fit to govern. We the people ignore their actions at our own peril. By embracing ignorance, by turning a blind eye and accepting the unacceptable, our moral compass is called into question.

Once state authorities legitimised the plunder of children belonging to Indigenous communities, they simply turned on another vulnerable section of the broader community. They began to remove thousands of babies from unwed mothers and fathers and placed them in the custody of government-appointed adoptive carers. Once again, this policy was deemed to be in the best interest of those children.

The grief suffered by both the children and their dispossessed families has been well-documented and apologies were eventually made for the cruel policies of the past. But yet again we failed to realise the full extent of the devastating policies and practices we were so profoundly involved in, and showed no remorse, compassion or empathy for the deep grief these vulnerable children and their powerless families experienced. And so, once more, we learnt absolutely nothing.

On and on the industry went, morphing into the present day cataclysm.

We at Family Briefing wondered how much media and political attention would be generated if one-in-four Australians were to unexpectedly find themselves threatened by rising seawater lapping at their front porches due to climate change. Would this not be the leading story of every news report for weeks, if not months? Yet the fact that one-in-four Australians is facing the prospect of being denied the protection of their biological family does not even raise an eyebrow let alone generate a single story.

We were yet to learn that, while morally indefensible, the redistribution of millions of children for profit is not new and has been considered perfectly legal for centuries. It beggars belief that the vast majority of the population remains unaware of the little known supreme guardianship powers of the state dating back to the 16th Century. These laws have continued to legitimise the forced removal of many generations of men, women and children from the protection of biological families, all at the hands of their own governments.

The combined number of those negatively impacted by the current 40- year-old child-removal policies of Australia, Canada, the UK and the US is staggering and has accumulated to an estimated 112 million people (adults and children) in the English-speaking world. Prevailing community ignorance is beyond comprehension, since once again, 21st Century governments are able to successfully convince their unsuspecting constituents that such removal of their children is actually in their best interest.

We were soon to learn however that we are already paying a heavy price for such community inertia. Contemporary family and child-protection laws, grossly unfit for purpose as they are, constitute an epic failure by all those complicit by their silence. Consequences will be calamitous.

Ignorant societies are setting future generations up to fail by weakening the social fabric of their communities and do so without blinking an eye. It is now highly unlikely that the next generation will be able to escape the inevitable turmoil created by these policies and preserve the social order that many enjoy so much but take for granted.

In the second decade of the millennium, a hyperventilating national media became totally preoccupied with the "marriage equality" rights of same-sex couples, a cohort less than one sixth of one per cent (0.16 per cent) of the civilian population. At the same time, completely ignored were the one in four, or 25 per cent (25 per cent) of the civilian population who have effectively been denied the equal right to the protection of their own biological family. With such double standards in defining "equality", are we deserving of nationhood?

That government created family and child-protection laws have served to trash the value and meaning of traditional marriage, is lost in the scramble for marriage equality rights. Shamefully, widespread evidence of a devalued public perception of marriage has also failed to pique the interest of all sides of secular politics, media and spiritual leadership.

We became more curious about what the possible social costs would be of current child-removal policies and if someone had even bothered to measure the full extent of the many horrendous consequences now burdening the still mainly law abiding citizens of contemporary civil societies, but who appear to be totally oblivious to what is going on.

And so we embarked on the search for another missing link.

It no longer came as a surprise, to discover that once again a comprehensive big picture overview, with the potential to provide the public and governments with an accurate assessment of the many negative societal consequences, is not readily available. It follows 40 years of apathy and inertia, which either by accident or design, serves to keep us safely in the dark.

Instead, smoke-and-mirror policies unfit for purpose rule the day and make a mockery of the once noble ideas of equality, justice and the rule of law.

By so doing and perhaps inadvertently, these policies are now major contributing influences on the slow demise of democracy itself. No one can come face to face with the brutality and hypocrisy of these systems and retain respect for the authorities who perpetuate them.

Discredited social policies faced by the population of contemporary Western democracies are reminiscent of the human-trafficking ideology of the slave trade that was also considered legitimate and allowed to inflict indescribable misery on a powerless minority for more than 300 years. The calls to bring a halt to those policies and practices and demand relief for the recipients of *their* horrific consequences were likewise completely ignored by the dominant white population of the time. And just as we witness today, any protestations from the anti-slavery movement were similarly shouted down and ridiculed by the powerful voices of those getting rich from the wretchedness of fellow members of the human family.

* * *

Before long, it became apparent that there are numerous ways to look at the societal cost of relationship breakdown. Especially since those costs are not only extensive, but because responsibility is also spread across a wide range of government departments and further complicated by the many layers of interconnected institutions and agencies.

Excessive drinking and substance abuse, domestic violence, the cost of family and children's courts, subsidised housing, high levels of unemployment and social dysfunction, even the cost in lost lives of those who suicide and their prevention programs as well as the long-term demographic impacts of low birth rates. All are consequences of widespread social-policy failure. They are also found in blowouts in welfare budgets and the personal costs in private pain as well as the stress induced medical and mental health issues, while the hidden social costs of forced warehousing of already damaged children in institutions are enormous. Furthermore, the ongoing lifetime costs to service the permanently damaged souls who were forced to survive deplorable childhoods, are seen in the cost to national education budgets as they battle to manage vulnerable children dealing with behavioural issues not of their own making. Not to forget the enormous law and order cost generated by the millions of dispossessed and victimised, who no longer have respect for the society that abandoned them as vulnerable children, which left them emotionally crippled.

All of these are factors in the government-created social cost blowouts of relationship breakdown in the Western world.

A system that rips children from the protective care of their biological parents with little or no cause is not a good system.

A system that gives one parent total power over the other and encourages prolonged and destructive disputation is not a good system.

The authorities know perfectly well that the current systems in place, lead to high welfare dependence among both men and women, long-lasting conflicts between separating couples, extremely high suicide rates, particularly among separated men, extremely poor outcomes and great emotional distress for children, as well as linked alcohol and substance abuse problems among both parents and children.

The failure to act is a craven lack of courage.

The marginalisation and denigration of those who dare to speak out, engineered by taxpayer-funded groups using well-honed disruptive tactics taken straight from supremacists' handbooks to shut down critical discussion, is shameful. The authorities know perfectly well, or should know perfectly well, that the institutions and processes that they created and now so piously protect, drive people to the brink, even to the extent of inducing psychotic episodes.

Many dispossessed parents suffer from Post-Traumatic Stress Disorder after losing their children, their property, their social standing, their savings, their dignity and self-respect, their incomes and, in many cases, even their personal freedom, as a result of the prolonged legal processes and child-removal practices associated with family breakdown.

The authorities are acutely aware of all of these factors, but instead of reforming the institutions and processes that are causing so much damage, they blame the victims and claim men and women who break down in this manner are either mentally ill or otherwise disadvantaged. Men who break down under extreme emotional duress and uncharacteristically commit terrible acts are all too often accused of being patriarchal abusers, women of being either mentally ill or the victims or even perpetrators of sustained abuse. In almost all cases, neither scenario is true.

It is the pre-existing knowledge that makes the failure to act and the deliberate storm of misinformation, deception and propaganda; and the extortionate funding of only one side of an ideologically charged argument; that makes the present circumstances so criminal.

Politicians have turned a blind eye for decades, but ultimately the truth will out.

The apologies that have been trotted out so frequently – for the Indigenous, for victims of institutional sex abuse, for the disinherited, for slavery – have become a devalued form of social ceremony or obeisance. A problem turned and faced will disappear. A problem ignored will follow you forever. The failure to confront these issues will ultimately turn on those perpetrating and protecting these practices.

Without adequate safeguards, foundations placed in a swamp will fail and the building placed on those foundations will ultimately sink and destroy itself.

Institutions created by incompetents using misinformation are founded on inadequate foundations and will also fail.

It is as if, in one analogy, a builder has built a house using a faulty spirit level. The house is built but the walls are not plumb and the floors are not level. Sooner or later the building will be condemned and eventually it will collapse, but who is to blame?

Is it the fault of the incompetent builder who failed to realize his spirit level was faulty?

Or the manufacturer of the faulty equipment?

Is it the fault of the builder who continues to use tools he knows, or should know, are defective?

Or is it the fault of the building inspector who accepted inferior work?

Or the owner who failed to check the credentials of the builder?

Or is it the wording of the building code that failed to provide adequate construction safeguards and protect the homeowners against dodgy builders, incompetent building inspectors or defective or malfunctioning equipment and materials?

Family and child-protection systems provide all the players and failings illustrated in the analogy of a failed building, with families and children the victims of failed systems that deserve universal condemnation. But, unless a credible circuit breaker is found to fix these difficulties, it is bound to continue to repeat itself.

We find ourselves in a terrible morass. It is our belief that if change is to occur, a unifying focus is needed to promote a dramatic shift to family and child protection, rather than continuing the highly charged emphasis on gender entitlement masquerading under the banner of "equality".

There are critical moments in history, turning points at which the distribution of factual information reaches critical mass and the penny drops and everyone begins to ask: Why have we allowed this to go on for so long?

* * *

One of the most striking things about the terrible outcome for the parents and children who have had control of their lives essentially seized by the state is that while millions of people are affected, discussion is minimal.

The outcome for the broader society may be disastrous, but genuine knowledge of how successive governments have allowed this situation to develop is almost non-existent.

Our lawmakers have become hostage to ideologies adopted by unthinking, self-perpetuating bureaucracies, peddling policies for the public that they would never countenance for their own children.

Meanwhile, the result of our own findings for 1975-2015 shows that on any given day, after 40 years of enduring legal oppression, an estimated one in four of the civilian population of Australia is being denied what we have identified and labelled as Protective Contact with their biological family. The cost to taxpayers is more each year than we spend on the whole of our annual defence budgets. We have learnt that waging war on ourselves in this way is made possible using oppressive legal systems, which are destroying millions, costing billions, offer no improvements, and ignore alternatives.

Fundamental human rights principles dictate that any legal system that ambushes the most vulnerable of a nation's citizens and crushes the life out of their human spirit does not deserve a place in a civilised society and should not be tolerated by any modern nation state. Yet, by ignoring the devastating consequences of just such a legal system and tolerating the brutal impact of contemporary family and child-protection laws, we collectively pretend not to notice the following comprehensively documented facts referenced in the well-sourced briefing papers of Family Briefing:[28]

- The unconditional requirement to ensure Protective Contact is maintained between immature children and the valuable protection presented by extended biological families
- The big picture data on family violence victims
- The 70% of suicides containing a family breakdown predictor
- The phenomena and number of socially radicalised children in lone-parent households
- The total number of citizens denied Protective Contact with their families

---

28 http://www.familybriefing.com/ – *One in Four of Us – The Numbers and the Costs –* 1975-2015

- The total economic and social costs of family breakdown and child protection
- The extremely poor quality and interconnected nature of a myriad of child-removal policies, laws and practices, which act as a catalyst for crippling health, social and economic outcomes
- The millions who self-medicate on drugs and alcohol, with a family breakdown predictor
- The 63% of teen suicides
- The 70% of juveniles in state-operated institutions
- The 71% of high school dropouts
- The 76% of children in chemical abuse centres
- The 85% of all youths in prison
- The 85% of children who exhibit behavioural disorders
- The 90% of homeless and runaway children
- The number of children placed in out-of-home care by State agencies.
- The State removing parental rights and assuming 16th Century supreme authority over the nation's children.
- The existence of vital 21st century child-protection alternatives.

In order to get an idea of the sheer scale of 21st Century child removals, one only has to consider the following estimated totals reached using the aforementioned methodology.

The 40-year total of the accumulated annual number of men, women and children denied the protection of their biological family is astonishing.

Each year, a similar number of dispossessed people are added, while around the same number drop off the radar due to the child reaching adulthood:

6 million – Australia	= 150,000 per year are added and vanish from statistics
9 million – Canada	= 225,000 per year are added and vanish from statistics
16 million – UK	= 400,000 per year are added and vanish from statistics
81 million – US	= 2,025,000 per year are added and vanish from statistics
112 million – Total	= 2.8 million added to the accumulated total each year

It is important to recognise that according to Government commissioned statistics, children account for around 30.7 per cent of the above numbers.

The fact that these discredited policies and practices, together with their well-documented consequences, provide a fertile breeding ground for exploitation by predatory individuals and institutional empire builders, to our mind constitutes criminal negligence by those within the highest echelons of government.

Paradoxically, the extensive service provider networks offering their services to help the victims of family and child protection policies accept their fate, are not only assigned to deal with the effects, but are also responsible for applying the very government laws and practices that trigger the prime causal factors in the first place. This is akin to the Gestapo offering to help the victims of the holocaust to accept their fate.

Those tasked with suicide prevention strategies for instance focus on finding ways to prevent suicide attempts being successful and repeatedly claim that the major causes leading to suicide are depression, PTSD and mental health issues. Not once do they refer to the existence of what may be one of the main underlying root causes of those conditions. This is particularly troubling, since gathering dust in the bottom drawer of a filing cabinet in a minister's office in the nation's capital, is an Australian study of 4,000 suicides commissioned back in 2000, which clearly indicates the overwhelming majority (70 per cent) had the common denominator of relationship breakdown as the primary causal factor.[29]

Likewise, those responsible for finding ways to reduce drug and alcohol dependency continue to focus on the effects and how to minimise them, rather than devoting attention to the elimination of root causes that can be shown to contribute to driving thousands of people into self-medicating addictions.

For many decades we have failed to question and uncritically accepted the often problematic narrative offered by family and child-protection ideologues.

Zealously advocating their cause and single-mindedly focused on expanding their power and influence, the child removers desperately need a constant flow of vulnerable children, your children, the nation's children. Without other people's children, their power and influence would be severely curtailed and, in many cases, their careers would grind to a halt.

The same relentless need for a steady flow of "vulnerable" children in order to secure and maintain their own existence, becomes obvious when intimidating conduct and behaviours are revealed during child protection, child support and domestic violence interventions.

To remain silent in the face of this human tragedy imposed in our name is unacceptable. One of the main objectives of this book therefore is to remove pleading ignorance as a viable excuse for failing to speak out.

---

29 Wesley Mission, *Suicide in Australia, a Dying Shame*. Sydney, 6 Nov. 2000.

Seven

The Economic Costs

THE BREAKDOWN OF relationships, whether married, cohabiting or never stably formed, has far-reaching costs. The emotional distress to those involved is considerable. The impact on children's life chances is profound. What is all too often either overlooked or deliberately downplayed, however, is the added economic cost burden to society as a whole.

That society has somehow allowed itself to be deceived into believing relationship breakdown is ably managed by means of carefully considered and well thought through government policies and must therefore be the very best we can do, is bad enough. The fact that the associated bourgeoning economic costs are also readily being accepted as justifiable is deeply troubling.

In a world that is struggling to live within its means and where budgetary cost blowouts generally come under close parliamentary scrutiny, the lack of questioning, transparency and accountability in our parliaments is mystifying.

Soul-destroying social policies that negatively impact more than 25 per cent of the civilian population and which are permitted to lawfully destroy the lives and futures of so many of the most vulnerable in our communities, go completely unchallenged by those who claim to represent the best interest of the electorate in our national parliaments.

The economic cost blowouts associated with failed social policies, likewise fail to pique the interest of those responsible for our economic security.

Equally difficult to comprehend is the extent of the community's lack of knowledge and the unmistakable media silence about the degree of chaos and economic destruction taking place in our name. This in turn has served to keep the electorate completely in the dark about the level of taxes they are paying to fund their own maltreatment.

Due to the endless demands of those advocating ever further expansion of the already dismally failing family and child-protection industry, enormous financial pressure has been added to our budgetary woes.

Bogged down and enfeebled by their lack of knowledge and understanding about the magnitude of deteriorating welfare and child-protection systems, those in charge of the nation's purse strings have little stomach for taking on the powerful family justice and child-protection lobby.

Emboldened by the success of their self-aggrandising campaigns which have served to provide them with a manufactured public image of authority and delivered significant influence in the corridors of power, this persuasive lobby is extremely well aware that their requests for extra funding are usually sympathetically met.

Single-mindedly, their attention is focussed on ever greater demands for taxpayer-funded financial support to prop up a perpetually growing, but chronically failing, social justice system and, by so doing, serve to impose an unsustainable budgetary cost burden on health, education, social services and criminal justice agencies, to name just a few.

The bureaucratic heavyweights, with their Machiavellian ways, know full well that the redistribution of children for profit, or what many now refer to as a system of government-sponsored child trafficking, has served to keep their proverbial proboscis deeply embedded in the public trough. Or perhaps they truly believe their own "Best Interests of the Child" propaganda.

What has been overlooked for generations is how this influential but morally offensive child-removal lobby has been able to contain the focus of public attention and effectively divert urgently needed scrutiny. Unless this situation is addressed and a counter-narrative produced, this socially destructive and economically unsustainable situation will continue unabated. Empires destroy people, and greed is a potent incentive for unsavoury practices. Our authorities often lie by commission and omission, covertly and overtly. It is the stories that are untold that so urgently need to be presented.

Despite concerted attempts to find the total annual taxpayer-funded costings of government expenditure on family and child-protection matters, these costings are either unavailable as a single expenditure item or are carefully buried within a host of other budgetary expenditure papers across a range of ministerial portfolios. This is made even more difficult with many of the economic costs spreading throughout a duplicated collection of state and federal portfolios, departments, institutions and agencies, as well as an assortment of NGOs and private for-profit corporations.

An additional hodgepodge of ambiguous legal definitions and unenforceable or non-existent minimum standards across national, state and territory borders, exacerbate the dismal outcome for children and families even further.

All of them are important contributing factors in the economic cost blowouts of relationship breakdown.

We were amazed at the impregnable cloak of secrecy that was being tolerated. Protected by a lack of transparency that serves to prevent scrutiny, a deceptive narrative has been created that offers an official explanation not even remotely resembling the truth.

Why are serious and probing questions not being asked by those responsible for protecting the nations' citizens? Why is the media so reluctant to challenge those that are unashamedly abusing the nations' taxpayers, families and children for economic gain? Why the government smokescreen? What could it possibly be that the government is so desperately trying to stop the electorate from finding out?

Our own research, however, had begun to unearth some interesting facts that would soon expose another missing link to help complete the overview we were endeavouring to produce.

The irony is that many governments, while often unintentionally, actually make a considerable amount of their official data available for public scrutiny. Open-source intelligence collection is now widely used by national intelligence agencies around the world, as a major source of information gathering. Eliminating much of the need for whistle-blowers, all that is required are committed investigators that have the time, passion, determination and patience.

Following along one of the well-worn lines of enquiry, we unexpectedly struck pay dirt. We opened a link and there it was. Readily accessible public information that confirmed our suspicions were well and truly warranted. It finally provided us with proof of the estimated economic cost to taxpayers of large-scale removal of children from their families and the existence of massive service-provider networks. The sheer scope and scale of these networks, which are being championed as heroically assisting traumatised children and their families cope with their heart wrenching loss, was astronomical.

The greatest upshot of this tragedy is that with very few exceptions, most countries spend considerably more of their GDP on waging war against their own citizens using family and child-protection laws than they spend on national defence budgets to safeguard their nation against external threats.

Until we came across a comprehensive British report that revealed the estimated price tag for relationship breakdown to the public purse, we had no idea what the overall cost burden to taxpayers might be. We soon came to understand, however, that this was not really surprising. A public left in the dark is easily duped into not questioning the reliability of political spin. We have yet to find another set of national economic data that would go anywhere near exposing the full extent of extortionate family and child protection budgetary expenditure as comprehensively as the British report has.

The Relationships Foundation is a British think-tank founded on the belief that a good society is built on good relationships, from family and community to public service and business. They study the effect that culture, business and government have on relationships and create new ideas for strengthening social connections and campaign on issues where relationships are being undermined.

The Foundation's apolitical approach goes way beyond traditional left-right political distinctions, allowing it to focus their attention on working with a wide range of leaders in business, academia, public service and politics to implement relational ideas.

The Foundation published its first estimate of the economic cost of family breakdown in its 2008 pamphlet *When Relationships Go Right/Wrong*. This formed the basis of a plea for a clear family policy that recognised both the extent of families' vital contribution to a wide range of policy objectives and the unsustainable costs of weak familial relationships.[30]

In 2009, the Foundation produced the first of its annual Cost of Family Failure indices, consisting of five main expenditure components. The latest updated index reveals that the 2016 cost of relationship breakdown to the British taxpayer, has increased for the seventh year in a row to a mind-blowing £48 billion (A$88 billion), up from £37 billion in 2009.[31]

These annual reports reveal that an estimated 500,000 British children and adults are drawn into the family-justice system each year. A British child born today may, on current trends, only have a 50/50 chance of living with both parents by the time they are 16 years old. A staggering 45 per cent of 15 year olds today are not living with both parents.

The British government has recognised the case for investment in their most troubled families and that the failure to support those fami-

---

30 Bingham, John. "Family Breakdown 'Could Cost Taxpayers £46bn.'" The Telegraph, 4 Mar. 2014, Accessed here: www.telegraph.co.uk/women/sex/divorce/10674267/Family-breakdown-could-cost-taxpayers-46bn.html.

31 Relationships Foundation, Cambridge CB4 2HY, Accessed here: http://www.relationshipsfoundation.org/counting-the-cost-of-family-failure-2016-update/

lies effectively undermines the life chances of children. The government's own figures calculate the 120,000 most troubled families alone cost £9 billion. Yet the same logic does not seem to have been applied to all families.

To put it in context, their earlier 2013 estimate of £46.07 billion revealed that this was equivalent to nearly 3 per cent of the UK's GDP based on nominal prices, 38 per cent of public sector net borrowing and 4 per cent of public sector net debt. It also showed that the relative sizes of the indices five components had remained stable over time. Health and social care remains the largest component of the five at 34 per cent, followed by tax and benefits, 30 per cent; civil and criminal justice, 18 per cent; housing, 11 per cent; and education and young people needs, 7 per cent. All five component areas of the index show a general upward trend since they began with their first edition in 2009. This has meant the average British taxpayer is now shouldering the economic cost burden to the tune of £1,820 a year.

The seven-year trend suggests that there are no signs these upward pressures on the cost to the public purse as a result of familial failure will abate in the near future.

As is the case elsewhere in Western democracies, despite some cuts to government spending on services dealing with the fallout from family breakdown, soaring rates of family failure and the catastrophic consequences of subsequent family and child-removal policies are tearing apart the social fabric.

The total cost of relationship breakdown to Australian taxpayers is more difficult to ascertain. Unlike the model available in the UK, there does not appear to be a complete costing model available in

Australia. Instead, we were forced to piece together four key expenditure components applicable to the Australian economy, consisting of reports on costings that are particularly relevant to relationship breakdown and which have been quoted by Government representatives on ad-hoc bases.

The first of these key expenditure components came to light as the result of an investigative newspaper report into at least some of the economic costs of relationship breakdown to the Australian economy.

In 2014, an exclusive News Corp Australia investigation found, that divorce and family breakdown were costing the national economy more than $14 billion a year in government assistance payments and court costs alone.[32]

It also found that over the previous two years, the cost of divorce to the national economy in those areas had increased by more than $2 billion dollars, or 17 per cent, with each Australian taxpayer paying about $1100 a year to support families in crisis. The News Corp analysis of information from the Federal Attorney General's department, the Department of Human Services and the Department of Social Services, showed in that financial year alone the government would spend $12.5 billion on support payments to single parents, including family tax benefits and rent assistance.

Another $1.5 billion would be spent on the administration of the child support system, while the cost to taxpayers from family disputes in Australian courts was $202 million. Almost 50,000 people get

---

[32] Wilson, Lauren, and Lisa Cornish. "Divorce Is Costing the Australian Economy $14 Billion a Year." *News.com.au*, News Limited, 5 July 2014, 10:52PM, Accessed here: www.news.com.au/lifestyle/relationships/marriage/divorce-is-costing-the-australian-economy-14-billion-a-year/news-story/e5a101ea76351d4ba145279011b934ac.

divorced each year in Australia, and while the divorce rate declined between 2002 and 2008, it is now on the rise again. The Minister in charge at the time, Kevin Andrews, who estimated that each divorce was costing Australian taxpayers at least $100,000, said understanding what divorce was costing the nation was important. "Whatever the figure comes out as, it is still a significant amount of money and I do think it is worth knowing because we are more likely to do more in terms of prevention," he said.

Here was the Federal minister responsible, virtually admitting that he had no idea what the total taxpayer-funded economic costs of relationship breakdown might be, yet acknowledging that he should be aware of what that amount actually was.

After all, how on earth can a minister possibly do more in terms of prevention if he has absolutely no idea what the extent of current socioeconomic costs are? How did he even think the success or failure of his governments' policies can be calculated, when governments don't have a starting benchmark figure against which to measure?

While less than 10 per cent of contested cases actually make it to trial for any number of reasons, the effects of family and child-protection policies have caused the forced removal of an estimated 6 million Australians from the protection of their families. That the exploitation of those policies are bound to have been for decades creating massive social upheaval and discontent in our communities, is not rocket science. Yet the situation has not warranted the urgent attention of our political leadership, who appear to prefer wasting time on infantile point-scoring, instead of tackling important social issues.

However, the resulting economic cost burden is equally staggering.

Added together, the massive socioeconomic costs should have sent alarm bells ringing throughout the hallowed halls of Western parliaments and alerted their long-suffering, unsuspecting communities long ago. The most likely reason these costs have failed to raise any alarms is because they have been carefully whitewashed from public scrutiny. Media editors find the whole area, beset as it is with suppression orders and ideological agenda, too difficult to cover and too polarising for their audiences; while those in charge of the national purse strings just want to keep the money flowing without drawing controversy.

It is difficult to see how any government can possibly create sound policies when the crucial information relied upon is so compromised as to make it worthless. As we discovered, the mutually related structure of complex interconnected networks also makes a big picture overview extremely difficult to formulate.

One explanation may be the fact that in a multibillion-dollar child-removal world, particularly one that offers ideologically aligned professional group's megadollar contracts to provide predetermined support for retaining the status quo, hired-gun report writers are not difficult to find.

And so we turned our attention to another key area of concern; that being the ever expanding cost blowout of one of the prime sectors driving the astronomical social and economic price tag of family and child-protection laws.

By far the biggest single contributor to those costs is the Family Violence sector which, enmeshed with its integrated networks, is sucking the lifeblood out of the Australian budget to the tune of $22 billion each year. To suggest that this sector is in urgent need of forensic scrutiny is a gross understatement. That this has not happened to date speaks volumes of the dire straits into which we have spiralled.

KPMG is a respected global network of professional services firms providing audit, tax and advisory services across a wide range of industries, including government ventures and the not-for-profit sector. The independent member firms of the KPMG network are affiliated with KPMG International Co-operative, which is a Swiss entity that takes great pride in its self-assessed, long tradition of professionalism and integrity. They proudly claim to offer deep expertise to help solve complex challenges and steer change.

Examined in recent reports prepared by KPMG regarding the economic cost of family violence in Australia, which were commissioned by both the Australian Department of Social Security and the Victorian Department of Premier and Cabinet during 2016 and 2017, the total estimated cost of family violence is costing Australia an astonishing $22 billion a year. [33] [34]

A civil society does not tolerate violence and abuse, period. Most particularly, there is a collective abhorrence to the abuse of children, with such abuses widely considered criminal acts, which need to be adjudicated in the criminal justice jurisdiction. Conversely, a civil society also does not readily support emotionally charged witch-hunts that take unfair advantage of ambiguous laws. There is widely held community distaste for laws that permit the targeting and exploitation of powerless family members in order to supply a perjuring plain-

---

[33] KPMG, "The Cost of Violence Against Women and their Children in Australia", May 2016

[34] KPMG , "The Cost of Family Violence in Victoria", May 2017

tiff with an unfair monetary or relationship advantage. Those targeted and falsely accused of violence and abuse, with absolute impunity, invariably end up losing their biological family, their life savings, and experience ongoing physical and emotional health issues for many years.

Much suspicion exists, therefore, about the credibility of the alleged extent of abuse, the exorbitant economic cost and the possible hidden motives for distortion of facts. The Family Violence sector is very well aware of the public distaste of abuse within the home and drives much of the populist discourse. But, as we were to learn in our investigations, there is much more to this publicly hyperventilated family violence component of family and child-protection systems than meets the eye.

The deliberate creation of what is known as "moral panic" within the community to further bureaucratic empire building, with no thought to the long-term consequences of these social policies, is a significant concern.

The next key component we considered particularly important.

Especially since nowhere else was total secrecy more evident than that preventing scrutiny of government funded child-protection services. As a major player in the child-removal sector, that there should be some identity protection goes without saying. But very little is known about the underlying reason for this almost paranoid insistence on a blanket information blackout in relation to the delicate subject of alleged child abuse and/or neglect.

Particularly so, when statistics suggest that such allegations far too often lead to the subsequent removal of children from their biological families.

This sector is most directly involved with the physical removal and housing of allegedly abused and neglected children. These are other people's children and the complete lack of transparency suggests there are issues at play of great concern to the dispossessed families and the whole of the community. The failure to provide information on the outcomes of government intervention into the lives of the nation's children demands urgent public attention.

A 2017 Productivity Commission document reports that the total recurrent economic cost of child protection, out-of-home care and family support services is costing Australian taxpayers around $4.8 billion per year.[35] The report says that since 2011-12, the national expenditure on child protection and out-of-home care services has shown an average annual increase of 3.9 per cent per year, with the most recent rise showing an increase of 7.7 per cent over the previous year. Of this expenditure, out-of-home care services accounted for the majority of those costs at 56.2 per cent, or $2.7 billion.

Evidence suggests many of the children taken into out-of-home care, are dispersed into regional areas where they serve to boost the local economy. The increased use of temporary accommodation and the creation of a range of new employment opportunities, funded by government child-removal agencies, have produced a growth in local social service industries that rely on a steady flow of other people's children. These children can end up isolated on rural properties, dotted around the regions, often thousands of kilometres from home.

---

35 Australian Government Productivity Commission. "Report on Government Services 2017", Vol. F, Ch. 16, Child Protection Services. 24 Jan. 2017. Accessed here: www.pc.gov.au/research/ongoing/report-on-government-services/2017/community-services/child-protection.

The underlying reason for paranoid secrecy around child protection and the out-of-home care delivered by government-funded service providers was to elude us for many years. We shared the frustration of many journalists who were silenced by suppression orders and threatened with prosecution should they dare to publish details of the child-protection system's failure. We were always sceptical of the official reasons given by governments for the concealment of details, but were at a loss to explain the real reason for such an extensive policy of cover-up.

That was until the birth family of missing Australian toddler William Tyrrell complained publicly about the government's insistence on keeping quiet for three long years and not reveal the real identity of Williams' birth family. For three years, this distraught family were forced to watch the infant boy's foster parents being presented as his biological parents. A News Corp Australia newspaper article by journalists Emily Richie and Rick Morton[36] reported that the biological grandmother of William, Ms Collins, complained about the determined efforts by the NSW government to keep his foster care status a secret. Allegedly, because of fears that publishing it might "stigmatise" him and his foster family, and that the public interest would not be satisfied. "They (the state government) have fought and fought and fought to keep this from the public and all the time we've had to sit there and watch another family pretend that William was their son," she said. "We watched them on television with their faces blurred and it hurt, it really hurt."

---

36 Richie, Emily and Morton, Rick, "William Tyrrell's Birth Family Say Government Secrecy May Have Cost Him His Fife", *The Australian*, 26 Aug. 2017.

"Nobody was interested in helping us get the truth out there, not even the police." Ms Collins also gave details about the lengthy negotiations between NSW Police and the Department of Family and Community Services when William disappeared, in particular about whether they could reveal the fact that he was in foster care. But, the refusal was upheld and the lid on public scrutiny of government policies remained shut.

So why would a government fight so hard to prevent the public from finding out about Williams' foster care status, we wondered. Not for the first time, we questioned why governments would insist on maintaining the dishonest public impression that the non-biological foster parents were actually Williams' biological parents? Why do governments repeatedly engage in such intensive attempts to cover up foster care status?

And then the penny dropped!

When children are in the legal care of their biological parents, their safety and well-being is the responsibility of those parents. If they fail to protect them from harm they will be held accountable for their failure to provide a safe environment for their children and face possible charges of abuse and/or neglect in the criminal justice jurisdiction.

Public knowledge is scarce however when it comes to knowing that, when government authorities remove children from their biological family using their 400-year-old parens patriae powers, the government becomes the legal parent and it is legally incumbent upon them to provide a safe environment for those children. If any government agencies or courts place them into an unsafe environment, they can be held legally accountable for failing to uphold their duty of care responsibilities and face extensive judicial enquiries, even Royal Commissions.

That it is beneficial for governments and their delegated agents to repeatedly lie to the public about who is legally responsible for the welfare of removed children in order to shirk the legal responsibility for their health and safety has become painfully evident.

This taxpayer-funded sector is obviously prepared to go to any length to hide the truth to protect their public funding, sector profile and personal careers. Even worse is the fact that they are eagerly supported by an extensive network of enabling institutions and agencies, all of which happen to be profiteering from the forced redistribution of other people's children.

The final of the four key components of a complex system of interrelated networks we considered to be in urgent need of closer examination was the economic costs of suicide to the Australian economy.

Much like the other components, this sector is protected by an almost impregnable wall of silence and protocols that effectively muzzle the media and silence its critics.

We soon discovered that reliable, comprehensive statistics on the economic costs and prime causal factors that trigger suicide are virtually impossible to obtain. While much research data is readily available, it is manifestly incomplete and conspicuous for the important and essential information left out. Lying to distort the facts can be achieved by either commission or omission. It is not difficult to understand why governments would consider it to not be in the public interest for the community to know why, how and by whom, so many of their loved ones are driven to take their own lives.

Professor Pierre Baume, founding dean of the Australian Institute for Suicide Research and Prevention at Griffith University in Queensland, found in a study of 4,000 suicides, that at least 70 per cent were associated with relationship break-ups.[37] This study also found men were nine times more likely than women to take their own lives following such break-ups.

Twenty-two years later and showing no signs of improvement in March 2016, the government released its latest ABS data, which clearly stated that death by suicide was continuing its upward trend in Australia and was at its highest rate in 10 years.[38]

We could not find another contributing risk factor for suicide anywhere, which was greater than the 70 per cent found in Professor Baume's study of 1994, yet somehow the single biggest contributing risk factor for suicide is never taken into account. A risk factor of 70 per cent that continues to be ignored throws a dark cloud of suspicion over the whole sorry state of the suicide-prevention sector. That successive governments have preferred to maintain a wall of silence around such information, soon became sickeningly obvious.

Taken over a period of 40 years, this 70 per cent statistic alone, translates into an estimated 65,000 Australians who may have been driven to take their own lives out of sheer desperation. These tortured souls had no defence against their government's persecutory policies

---

37 Baume, Pierre J.M., "Developing a National Suicide Strategy for Australia". In *Public Health Significance of Suicide: Prevention Strategies*. Proceedings of the National Conference on Public Health: Significance of Suicide, Lakeside Hotel, Canberra, 28 Feb. to 1 Mar. 1994.

38 National Mental Health Commission, "Suicide in Australia – 2014 Causes of Death Data (ABS)" (Australian Bureau of Statistics). Accessed here: http://www.mentalhealthcommission.gov.au/media-centre/news/suicide-in-australia-%E2%80%93-2014-causes-of-death-data-(abs).aspx

that denied them the protection of their family and served to destroy important family kinship bonds following relationship breakdown. Many thousands of our grief-stricken families, friends, neighbours and Aboriginal brothers and sisters, took their own lives out of utter despair at the hopelessness of their situation. United in grief, they paid the ultimate price for our ignorance.

Tens of thousands of Australian men, women and children pushed far beyond the brink of their endurance, for an ideology we cannot talk about without being tarred and feathered.

By refusing to question what soul-destroying psychological pressure is being applied to extinguish the emotional well-being of those of our family, friends and neighbours who suffer relationship breakdown, we ensure that most of us will remain totally unprepared for the dreaded knock when it reverberates on our own door. And so the counting continues unabated.

While no doubt most are well-intentioned, the vast majority of those tasked with suicide prevention appear not to realise they are basically used to serve as ambulances at the bottom of the cliff, waiting for other sectors of government-sponsored family and child-removal agencies to push helpless, disempowered and dispossessed targets over the cliff.

Suicide has been estimated to cost the Australian economy $17.5 billion per year by a group of respected leading national organisations involved in every aspect of suicide prevention.

In their comprehensive 2010 report, Breaking the Silence,[39] John

---

39 Mendoza, John, and Rosenberg, Sebastian, *Suicide and Suicide Prevention in Australia: Breaking the Silence*. Initiated by Lifeline Australia and Suicide Prevention Australia et al, 2010. https://www.lifeline.org.au/static/uploads/files/breaking-the-silence-secured-wfbcyutdeukg.pdf

Mendoza and Sebastian Rosenberg, pointed out that for every person who takes their own life, another 25 tormented individuals engage in failed attempts to do so, with half of those requiring hospitalisation.

We acknowledge and respect that there are many sad and unavoidable reasons that cause a number of troubled people to take their own lives, no matter how hard a caring community might try to prevent such events.

For the purpose of this book, however, we are most particularly interested in determining the dreadful impact of chronic government policy failure within the context of child protection and family law and therefore focus our concerns on the conceivably preventable 70 per cent of suicides that have been found to share a common risk factor – relationship breakdown. When what appears likely to be the biggest single contributing risk factor in terms of lives lost continues to be completely ignored and the focus remains on a range of consequences instead of prime causal factors by those engaged in formulating suicide prevention strategies, suicide numbers are unlikely to come down anytime soon.

Since the silence has not been broken and unacceptably high rates of suicide continue their upward trend, it suggests that the influence of dominant voices dictating the enforced silence on suicide prevention failure continue to hold the balance of power at the highest level of government and bureaucracy.

The portion that no one wants to talk about, the 70 per cent related to relationship breakdown, comes to an estimated annual cost of $12.2 billion out of a total of $17.5 billion. Since the way this society deals with relationship breakdown is entirely driven by government policy, this is a largely avoidable impost on the national economy.

Imagine what would happen if those tasked with finding ways to prevent malignant cancers from developing were prohibited by vested interests from considering or even mentioning the effects of smoking, asbestos or sun exposure? Alternatively, what would be the community response if vested interests were allowed to dictate to those tasked with reducing the national road toll that excessive speed, drink-driving or running red lights were not allowed to be considered as primary risk factors?

The combined total estimated cost of the four key expenditure components of this one sector of our economy alone, accounts for an astonishing taxpayer-funded budgetary drain of $53 billion a year, which in 2017 equates to a staggering 3.46 per cent of Australia's GDP.

Those applying the cure have now become captive to the economic treasure trove of government funding that supports their actions. As a result, removing children from the protection of their family for profit has become a problem in itself due to its addictive qualities, and has turned it into a devastating community problem.

Finally, to illustrate the full extent of the budgetary drain on Australia's economy caused by chronically failing family and child-protection policy outcomes, we positioned their combined estimated cost to Australian taxpayers, within the context of the value of earnings of Australia's top export-earning industries in Australian dollar terms.[40]

Incredibly, at a total annual cost of $53 billion, the cost of relation-

---

40 Office of the Chief Economist, Department of Industry, Innovation and Science, "Australian Industry Report 2016", Ch. 2, Economic Conditions, p25. https://industry.gov.au/Office-of-the-Chief-Economist/Publications/AustralianIndustryReport/assets/Australian-Industry-Report-2016.pdf

ship breakdown and the associated taxpayer-funded industries was $5.3 billion more than the whole of the dollar value of Australia's top export earner in 2015-2016, iron ore at $47.7 billion.

Measured another way, at an estimated total annual cost of $53 billion, government expenditure on the maltreatment of its own citizens is costing the nation $18.7 billion more each year than it earns from its second largest export earner, coal, which in 2016 earned the nation $34.3 billion.

The total annual cost of $53 billion can also be measured as costing Australian taxpayers $15.5 billion more than the combined export earnings of the third and fourth largest Australian exports at $37.5 billion, those being education at $21 billion and natural gas at $16.5 billion.

Another disconcerting comparison can be made when the expenditure on child-removal policies is compared with national defence spending. While the Australian government is prepared to throw $53 billion each year at worsening child-protection policies, current budgetary priorities indicate it is only prepared to spend $34.6 billion on defence of the nation against external threats.[41]

For an important international perspective, it is also well worth considering the widespread economic implications to other national budget bottom lines.

We used the same methodology as we used to calculate the costs in Australia and applied them to Canada, the UK and the US, all of which have child-removal practices that are very similar to those of Australia.

---

41 Budget 2017-2018, Defence Budget Overview, Department of Defence Ministers, May 9, 2017

Subject to exchange rates, and based on the approximate size of their 2018 populations, the estimated budgetary cost of family breakdown and child protection each year, measured in Australian dollars, is calculated as follows.

Australia	= $53.0 billion annually
Canada	= $79.5 ....
UK	= $145.75 ....
US	= $715.5 ....
Total in Aus. Dollars	= $993.75 billion annually

Note these amounts exclude the large amounts of private funds extracted from embattled families, or a country's lost production costs resulting from the economic, physical and emotional exhaustion suffered by those ambushed by the system.

In recent years, the political leadership of these four rich and powerful nations have lined up to shed crocodile tears and make apologies for the cruelty their predecessors inflicted upon their constituents by past practices of removing children from the protection of their families.[42]

The hypocrisy of their apologies becomes even more objectionable, however, with the spectacle of the pious sanctioning of their own child-removal policies, which in fact mirror those of their predecessors.

We cannot escape complicity. By acting like lambs led to slaughter and tolerating dispossession policies similar to those used in the past and by failing to question incompetence and deception, we are the enablers that fail the nation's children and allow the unprincipled to rule the day.

---

42 www.familybriefing.com, *Children of the State,* (MP3) Parts 1, 2, 3, and 4.

Is it possible that such staggering costs are justifiable? Are there perhaps some encouraging signs of an evolving pattern of improvement? It seems not! After 40 years, there is not a single sign of any reducing trend in any of the following disturbing family breakdown related areas:
- Child and family removal numbers
- Family-breakdown-related social and economic costs
- Family violence numbers
- Family-breakdown-related suicides
- Socially radicalised children
- Self-medicating drug and alcohol abuse
- Deaths, injuries and neglect in single-parent households

So the question remains unanswered: Who exactly are the beneficiaries of a system that destroys millions, costs billions, offers no social benefits, does not improve the lives of individuals and ignores alternatives?

It is, literally, an industry built on human misery. Like the slave trade of old, many have grown wealthy from it. And, those thus enriched and conscience free, living in self-reinforcing bubbles of opinion divorced from facts, have no motivation to fix the problems from which they so manifestly benefit.

Eight

The Root Cause and Integrated Networks

FAMILY BRIEFING had reached a stage where the overwhelming evidence indicated the difficulties faced by unsuspecting communities were far bigger than we could ever have imagined. While it became increasingly obvious that the extent of the lies told and incompetence displayed by authorities defied belief, they nevertheless serve to prop up a complex, interconnected system of national and international child-removal networks on a scale not seen before in modern history. Its reach is worldwide and the stakes are high for those engaged in profiting from other peoples' children.

Globally, we witness monumental policy stuff-ups in child protection, fire protection, intelligence protection and more recently the lack of protection from a predatory financial services sector. Ill-conceived legislation produced by incompetent, seat-warming legislators elected by a confused and disillusioned electorate, has placed many lives at risk. Following years of community silence, our collective complacency and willingness to ignore decades of industry warnings, is beginning to show signs of consequence. Irreparable damage has been done and the die is now cast.

The Grenfell Tower inferno in London[43] and subsequent Australian Broadcasting Corporation reports demonstrated clearly that fire-protection laws are not fit for purpose and have exposed gross government negligence caused by poorly drafted legislation.[44] Widespread policy exploitation has now distributed the equivalent of several containers of highly flammable liquid throughout the homes of millions of unsuspecting property owners and placed countless lives in jeopardy in the process.

Future Royal Commissions and coronial enquiries are sure to condemn governments for their negligence in drafting laws that claim, but fail, to protect. The disastrous outcome for victims of fire-protection laws that lack teeth, bear an uncomfortable resemblance to the lethal consequences suffered by the victims of family and child-protection laws.

Mirroring their deadly counterparts in the family justice jurisdiction, impotent fire protection and financial services protection laws riddled with legal loopholes, lack effective compliance enforcement protocols, provide no actual punishment for wrongdoing and so fail to protect the public from widespread institutional abuse. Managed by ill-informed and arrogant authorities who have ignored dire warnings expressed by concerned industry leaders, have resulted in years of irresponsible behaviour by those exploiting policy weakness for profit.

Successive governments in many parts of the world, who have

---

43 ABC News (Australia), "Grenfell Tower: Cladding on Dozens of UK Apartment Blocks Fails Fire Safety Tests after London Inferno", 25 June 2017, www.abc.net.au/news/2017-06-24/grenfell-tower-34-uk-high-rises-fail-cladding-tests/8649342. From an Associated Press story

44 Whitmont, Debbie, and Sarah Ferguson. "Combustible." *Four Corners*, ABC News (Australia), 31 Aug. 2017, 12:26pm, Accessed here: www.abc.net.au/4corners/combustible/8859420.

ignored the evidence of extensive negative consequences, are likely to face criminal negligence charges.

So how is all this made possible we wondered? How on earth can so many national governments expose so many families and children to so much danger over so many decades? Who is responsible for creating impotent family and child-protection legislation and how does the legislation fail to protect the general population? Who exploits the many legal loopholes in the legislation and how is that accomplished? What are some of the major consequences? How do countless service-provider networks all feed off one another, and who is to be held accountable for destroying so many lives over so many years?

Government statistics indicate that we have allowed the forced removal of many millions of "protective" family members from their biological children, and have stood by silently and watched while they were replaced by thousands of civil servants and a collective of profiteering, enabling cohorts who now decide what is best for the nation's children.

There are many reasons why this has been tolerated for so long, but primarily it happens due to the financial gains that family breakdown presents, and because not one of the many contributing factors operates in isolation.

They are all interconnected, creating the biggest, costliest, least effective and most damaging child-protection networks the world has witnessed. The enormity of the social and economic costs and the sheer magnitude of the number of people harmfully impacted, causing many to take their own lives, has the potential to lead to a dangerous erosion of confidence in our political leadership and in so doing, democracy itself.

The underlying root cause for the destructive mayhem inflicted on an unsuspecting electorate however, is the Orwellian legislation that legitimises the redistribution of children for profit and serves to appease the personal power agendas of the exploiters.

Matching some of the worst human rights abuses in human history inflicted by the dominant societal group upon their fellow human beings, current family and child-protection laws, morally indefensible by any measure of human decency, continue to enjoy the support of the national governments of our time. For their brutality and horror alone, they rate alongside the cruelty inflicted by the slave trading nations of the world upon the powerless victims at the source of *their* human trade.

To demonstrate how insidiously the system operates, our next challenge was to find a way to show what made it all possible. By this time, Family Briefing had become acutely aware that to draw attention to the resulting devastating consequences, a way had to be found to illustrate the complexities of the system in an easy to understand format.

Following a great deal of experimentation, we were eventually able to produce a visual aid showing the sequence of movement, actions and activities of the many people involved in a complex legitimised child-removal system. After a good deal of work, we successfully demonstrated how all the key components of family and child-protection laws are interconnected and share in the profitable pursuit of children for removal. The diagram clearly illustrates why and how these international laws and their procedural legal loopholes fail to protect millions of 21st Century children from being removed from their biological families, and incontrovertibly serves to identify the catalyst for the horror that follows.

The following flowchart illustrates the multifarious web of interrelated institutions and agencies responsible:

Full size copies are available at the Family Briefing website.

FAMILY BREAKDOWN – CHILD PROTECTION – CHILD REMOVAL – 1975-2015

HOW ALL THE KEY COMPONENTS OF FAMILY LAW AND CHILD PROTECTION LAWS ARE INTERCONNECTED

AND

WHY AND HOW INTERNATIONAL FAMILY LAWS AND PROCEDURAL LEGAL LOOPHOLES, FAIL TO PROTECT FAMILIES AND CHILDREN.

FUNDAMENTALLY FLAWED STATUTES PROVIDE

- No Legal Parenting Rights
- No Mandatory Mental Health Screening
- Secrecy Provisions
- Non-Enforcement of Contact Orders
- No Penalty for False Allegations
- Discriminating Power Differential Bias *
- Ambiguous, Problematic Terminology **
- Low Burden of Proof
- No Familial Protection ***

ENCOURAGED BY IMPUNITY AND REWARDING OF PERPETRATORS, WIDESPREAD USE OF THE FOLLOWING CRIMINAL OFFENCES ENSUES

- Perjury
- Perverting the Course of Justice
- Contempt of Court
- Fraud
- Child Abduction
- Child Abuse
- Radicalising/Inciting Prejudicial Hate

FURTHER COMPOUNDED BY THE SANCTIONING OF SOME QUESTIONABLE PRACTICES AND FAILINGS BY SELECTED GOVERNMENT AGENCIES

- Child Support Agencies
- Family Violence Agencies
- Child Protection Agencies
- Child Adoption Agencies

© www.familybriefing.com 2014

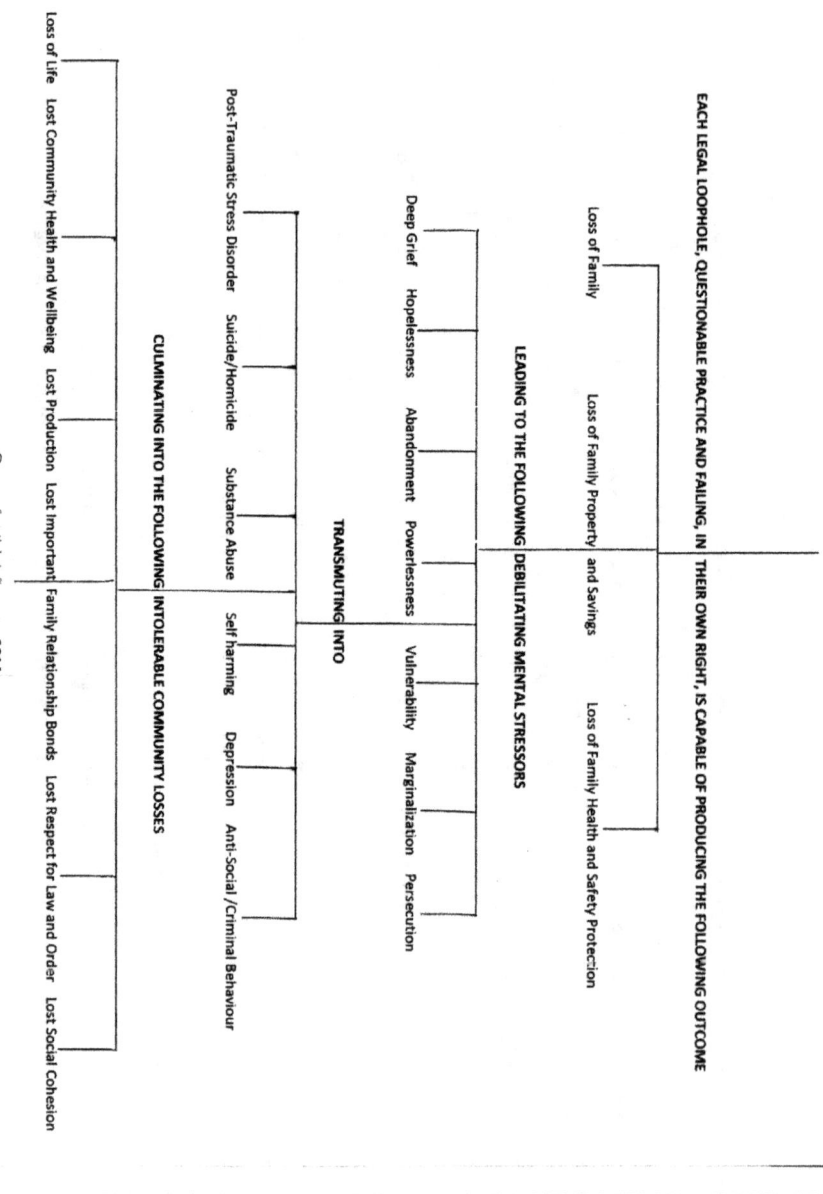

CHILDREN OF THE STATE

LARGELY FOUNDED ON INCORRECT OR MISLEADING DATA, PRODUCED AND PRESENTED AS FACT BY GOVERNMENT FUNDED

- Industry Ideologues
- Partisan Academic Researchers
- Beneficiary Stakeholder Groups

ALL MADE POSSIBLE BY UNQUESTIONINGLY ACCEPTING MISINFORMATION AS FACT, AND SUBSEQUENT FAILURE TO ACT APPROPRIATELY DUE TO

- Community Apathy
- Media Priorities
- Political Expediency

ULTIMATELY CONCLUDING IN THE FOLLOWING TAXPAYER FUNDED

CRIPPLING PUBLIC HEALTH CARE AND LAW AND ORDER COSTS AND COMMUNITY WELFARE EXPENDITURES

* **Discriminating Power Differential Bias:** While there certainly is evidence of gender bias, by far the worst example of discriminatory bias is in the Parental Status bestowed on the parents. Making one the Primary Parent and the other a Secondary Parent, in practice delivers total control over every parenting aspect to the Primary Parent and renders the Secondary Parent impotent. Such unconstrained power differential controls are continued in the ensuing Primary Parent/Child relationship, with devastating outcomes for the Child and the Secondary Parent.

** **Ambiguous, Problematic Terminology:** Contemporary family law systems are built on judicial discretion, which means that unfettered by guidelines, identical cases can have very different outcomes in different courts between different judges. Ambiguous and problematic guiding principles such as "Best Interest of the Child", "Equal Shared Parenting", "Meaningful Relationship", "Regular Involvement", "Equal Shared Responsibility", "Fitness to Parent" are all on offer, but are meaningless, and in the end the outcome will simply depend on the ideology or mood of the Judge on the day. Ask 20 different Judges their interpretation of "Best", "Equal", "Meaningful", "Shared", "Regular" and "Fitness", and you will receive 20 different answers.

*** **No Familial Protection:** Unlike the "Hague Convention", contemporary Family Laws allow a dysfunctional parent to lodge a false abuse claim against the other parent with impunity and so remove that parent from his/her child. Irrespective of the eventual outcome of the abuse claim, such time alone with the child is used to radicalize the child's thought processes against the absent parent. Subsequently, such primary care living arrangements are generally rubber stamped by the judiciary in final orders.

© www.familybriefing.com 2014

Following extensive analysis of publicly available material, and by applying our Protective Contact benchmark in combination with UK and Australian costings for modelling purposes, we were able to develop an up to date data set that would enhance quality policy development. It had become obvious that at the core of societies' maltreatment are fundamentally flawed laws that embolden the slow obliteration of our social structure.

A different set of values and different laws would provide the community with a more equitable outcome, so why have successive governments tolerated such destruction for so long?

Unfettered self-interest of the political and legal castes, using outdated ideologies acquired at the knees of their professors as justification, means they operate against the interests of the general public – and get away with it.

Political leadership of the developed world are fond of proclaiming they govern a country of laws and, with great pride, our lawmakers then declare their unquestioning belief in the rule of law. It is intended to make them appear principled, and serves to make the electorate feel safe in the knowledge that our country's laws will protect us from harm. In the main they certainly do, but it also functions to discourage their constituents from questioning the validity of such broad assertions.

So what do we really know about these laws? How well do they actually protect us and from whom exactly?

Upon closer examination of family and child protection laws, a disturbing picture emerges of a plethora of legal loopholes and unscrupulous actions. Not only are these being condoned, but often encouraged in order to undermine the intended purpose of delivering a just outcome for the nation's children and their families in our courts of law.

Many of these unprincipled activities, combined with legal loopholes you can drive a truck through, border on corrupt practices intended to subvert justice itself. Family Court secrecy prevents scrutiny, but in due course manifest malfeasance in this jurisdiction will be exposed.

Not only must justice be done, it must also be seen to be done.[45] This paraphrased almost century-old rule of law principle states that the mere appearance of bias is sufficient to overturn a judicial decision.

So, what is the rule of law?

Internationally accepted standards dictate that in order to uphold the rule of law, the following system of four universal principles need to be observed.

- That all governments and their officials and agents as well as individuals and private entities are accountable under the law.
- That all laws are clear, publicised, stable and just, are applied evenly and protect fundamental rights, including the security of persons and property and certain core human rights.
- That the process, by which the laws are enacted, administered and enforced is accessible, fair and efficient.
- That justice is delivered timely by competent, ethical and independent representatives who are neutral, are of sufficient number, have adequate resources and reflect the make-up of the communities they serve.

---

45 The full principle is stated in the 1924 English case, *Rex v Sussex Justices; Ex parte McCarthy*, "It is not merely of some importance but is of fundamental importance, that justice should not only be done, but must manifestly and undoubtedly be seen to be done." Lord Hewart CJ, quoted by then NSW Chief Justice Jim Spigelman in his keynote address to the 31st Australian Legal Convention, Canberra, October 1999.

The main function of the rule of law is to protect the lives, liberties, rights and property of citizens. There are two fundamental areas of law: criminal law and civil law. These are two broad and separate divisions of law with separate sets of laws and punishments.

William Geldart wrote in his standard account *Introduction to English Law*: "The difference between civil law and criminal law turns on the difference between two different objects which law seeks to pursue – redress or punishment. The object of civil law is the redress of wrongs by compelling compensation or restitution: the wrongdoer is not punished; he/she[46] only suffers so much harm as is necessary to make good the wrong he/she has done. The person who has suffered gets a definite benefit from the law, or at least avoids a loss.

"On the other hand, in the case of crimes, the main object of the law is to punish the wrongdoer; to give him/her and others a strong inducement not to commit same or similar crimes, to reform him/her if possible and perhaps to satisfy the public sense that wrongdoing ought to meet with retribution."[47]

In simple terms, criminal law refers to:
- Laws that are defined by legislation, enforced by the police and prosecuted by the state.
- Laws that set clear and firm boundaries of conduct for acceptable individual behaviour in society.
- The burden of proof lies with the government and the standard is "Beyond a reasonable doubt" or approximately more than 99%.

---

46 "He/she" pronouns are used at author's discretion here and do not appear in the original text.

47 Geldart, William M. *Introduction to English Law*. Edited by Yardley C.M. David, 9th ed., Oxford University Press, 1984.

- If found guilty, a person is punishable by either incarceration in prison, a fine or in some instances the death penalty.

Civil law on the other hand refers to:
- Laws that commence with a complaint being filed by one party called the plaintiff against another party called the defendant and the process is called litigation. Family law is settled in civil courts.
- In civil litigation the plaintiff is asking the court to order the defendant to remedy a wrong and outcomes are rarely enforced.
- The burden of proof lies with the plaintiff and then with the defendant to refute the evidence provided by the plaintiff. The standard is "On the balance of probability" or more than 50%.
- In family law litigation, a wrongdoing defendant is not punished and any contact or access orders a court makes in favour of a non-custodial plaintiff, are rarely enforced by the state.

There are many broad differences between criminal and civil laws.

One of the most disturbing aspects of family justice legislation is the way in which a considerable number of criminal actions by litigating parties are not considered crimes when adjudicated in civil courts. Consequently, they are exploited at will by many litigants and make a mockery of the justice system.

While there certainly is evidence of gender bias, by far the worst example of discriminatory bias is in the parental status bestowed on the parents. Making one the primary parent and the other a secondary parent in practice delivers total control over every parenting aspect to the primary parent and renders the secondary parent impotent. Such unconstrained power differentials are invariably continued into the subsequent primary parent/child relationship, with devastating outcomes for both the child and the absent secondary parent.

Contemporary family law systems are built on judicial discretion, which means that unfettered by clear guidelines, identical cases can have very different outcomes in different courts between different judges.

Ambiguous and problematic guiding principles such as "Best Interest of the Child", "Equal Shared Parenting", "Meaningful Relationship", "Regular Involvement", "Equal Shared Responsibility", "Fitness to Parent" are all on offer, but are meaningless, and in the end the outcome will simply depend on the ideology or mood of the judge on the day. Ask 20 judges their interpretations of "Best", "Equal", "Meaningful", "Shared", "Regular" and "Fitness", and you will receive 20 different answers.

Unlike the Hague Convention, contemporary family laws allow a vexatious parent to lodge a false abuse claim against the other parent with absolute impunity and so remove that parent from his/her child. Irrespective of the eventual outcome of the abuse claim, such time alone with the child is invariably used to radicalise the child's thought processes against the absent parent. Customarily, such primary care living arrangements, with the often disturbed parent or guardian, are subsequently rubber stamped by the judiciary in final orders. Such judicial expediency abandons far too many minor children into horrendous situations, leaving them without anyone to turn to for protection.

One citizen denounces another citizen for a horrific crime.

The accused is assumed to be guilty until the trial.

The onus of proof is on the accused.

At the trial the standard of proof is not beyond reasonable doubt; not on the balance of probabilities; but lingering doubts in the mind of the judge.

The punishment of the guilty is denial of access to their child.

There is seldom exoneration of the innocent.

This court of law has become a gross abuser of human rights.[48]

The most troubling of all is the fact that any contact visitation orders obtained in family courts, often at great expense to the litigants, will not be enforced by the courts. This fact alone illustrates the absolute futility of the whole exercise and generally comes as a rude shock to those desperately searching for a legal right to protect their biological children from harm.

To suffer the loss of a child strikes deeper into the human heart than anything else. Instinctively, parents will do anything to avoid losing their child or to prevent it suffering. This can be seen in the way parents who can't swim will dive into deep water to save their drowning child or in their willingness to present themselves in exchange for the freedom of their child if held hostage.

However on the dark side, there is also an inherent awareness that in order to inflict the most crippling pain on someone, this can be achieved by removing or harming their children. In order to provide protection for our children, we also have a natural inbuilt moral code of conduct that binds us together in a commonality to protect all of humanities' children.

---

48 Hirst, John, *Kangaroo Court: Family Law in Australia*, Quarterly Essay, Issue 17, 2005.

Collectively, as a civilised community, we possess a strong sense of humanity's justice for all and the need to support the rule of law in principle.

Accordingly, society has created and overwhelmingly embraced a set of criminal laws that ensure anyone harming children will be severely punished. These laws make it a criminal offence to injure, neglect or kidnap a child. Severe penalties apply to those committing the criminal offences of perjury and/or perverting the course of justice and/or are in contempt of court, in all matters relating to activities that lead to the abduction and keeping of a child in captivity as a hostage. The community feels safe in the knowledge that our criminal laws will protect its children from harm and will punish anyone breaking those laws.

Unfortunately, the community's blind trust in the family justice jurisdiction is thoroughly misplaced. Since nothing could be further from the truth, it is incumbent on all decent people therefore to learn the truth and be made aware that matters relating to parental child removals are not adjudicated in the criminal courts but in civil courts. In the jurisdiction of civil law, a totally different set of rules apply whereby perjury, contempt of court, perverting the course of justice and parental kidnapping go unpunished and are often rewarded. Anyone who makes a pre-emptive first strike will generally win all.

Also not well understood is how, by appealing to a family court or any government agency for assistance to help sort out parenting, child custody or contact matters, prospective litigants or fatigued parents admit either conflict or a lack of coping skills exist. This is seen as an admission of parental failure, categorises the children as vulnerable, and automatically enters those children on a potential watch list for future removal from their family.

Not for a moment is it suggested that no relationship should be allowed to fail. It is part of the human condition that some inevitably will fail and it is likewise accepted that for most people the experience is extremely painful. The problem is how these vulnerable families and their powerless children have been allowed to become cash cows to be milked by a government-created network of institutional bullies, who prey on their vulnerability and target them for their economic value.

An analogy of the redistribution of children for profit big picture is that of a deadly spider weaving a sticky web consisting of many threads with which to catch its doomed prey. Waiting in the centre of the web for its victims to get caught in any one of the many equally deadly sticky threads is the architect and creator of the web. Armed with the power of life and death over its victims, the creator has also become judge, jury and executioner of those caught in its web.

National governments, acting in their legal capacity as supreme guardians of the vulnerable, have become that deadly spider and have been allowed to create a range of institutional networks of deadly webs. Once caught in any one of those interconnected threads, the nightmare begins and you are soon engaged in a fight you cannot win.

Your life will spiral into depths of despair the likes of which you have never encountered before and soon you will discover that the only help available is that provided by another appendage, such as counselling services, of the very same system that has captured you in the first place.

Once trapped in the system, for children and their powerless families, there is no escape, period.

Unfortunately, these outcomes are taking place on a grand scale with frightening ease and speed, and are by no means unique to Australia. As we have shown in the supporting data from the US, Canada and the UK, there are considerable worldwide implications.

For far too long governments have unquestioningly accepted a steady diet of deceptive half-truths and deliberate misinformation provided by self-serving industry ideologues in order to justify their formulation of family and child-removal policies. They are only listening to one side of the story. The voices of those most directly affected are invariably ignored.

The following small glimpse into the covert efforts to influence government-supported bigotry and gender prejudiced attitudes by stealth, is also well worth noting.

During his 16-year reign acting as chief protector of Australian children, the former Chief Justice of the Family Court, Alastair Nicholson, presided over the systemic, involuntary removal of an estimated 736,000 children from "Protective Contact" with their families. His preening displays of gender prejudice, slavish devotion to anti-nuclear family ideologies and lack of impartiality became painfully evident in 1998.

It was during a protracted national debate on shared parenting and the multiple dysfunctions of his widely despised court that he referred to any desperate fathers who tried in vain to remain in Protective Contact with their children as "sinister men" who wanted to change the law to disadvantage women. He accused them of exhibiting a complete absence of concern for their children, other than as objects of their rights and entitlements.[49]

---

[49] Milburn, Caroline. "Family Court Chief Raps 'Sinister Men.'" *The Age* (Melbourne), 21 Oct. 1998,

Many people have pointed out how such taxpayer funded gender bigotry is alive and well today and claim that the "Sinister Men using children as objects of rights and entitlements" mentality which Nicholson speaks of is psychological projection craftily misdirected.

Attention is drawn to the steadily increasing use of the deceptive phrase *"Violence against women and their children"*, which has now become the main thrust of the fake narrative supporting discredited child-removal processes.

The hypocrisy of mothers claiming ownership of children while fathers are cast as violent and sinister miscreant's, leaves no doubt about who is using children as objects of entitlement.

A little known fact is that nowhere in Family Law legislation, can parents claim any legal ownership of their biological children; since a 400-year-old parens patriae authority decrees a nation's children belong to the state. However, while most people remain under the false impression they have a legal right to parent their own biological children according to how it serves their children's best interest, such naive impression will continue to serve as a catalyst to drive them into the waiting clutches of state-supported, profit-driven child-removal systems.

Sixteen years later, in *The Age* newspaper, the same Alastair Nicholson, who by then had been able to position himself as the chairman of Children's Rights International, proclaims that he is "ashamed of being an Australian". He was speaking in the context of a fierce controversy over the treatment of refugees. Ironically, and perhaps a sign of things to come, many people now consider the bigoted attitude and actions of one of his predecessors tasked with managing another vulnerable dispossessed minority, the Chief Protector of Aboriginals, the most notorious being the widely feared Auber Neville, a historical embarrassment.[50]

Draconian family and child-protection legislation, brutally applied in government institutions, has attracted many critics over the years, from within and outside of the legal fraternity. Many continue to call for the dismantling of a broken justice system not considered fit for purpose in the 21st Century. They point to the way secrecy provisions, suppression orders, freedom of information laws and the "best interest of children" criterion, protects a system of cruelty, the brutality of which we have not seen before, and call for those responsible to be held accountable.

Without any legal parenting rights, once their journey into the legal quagmire begins, families are at the mercy of those ready to exploit the system for profit. There are no winners apart from those engaged in plundering the family's financial resources and the family's children. Like slaughtered lambs, families are fleeced, drawn and quartered.

As one British law lecturer, who wishes to remain anonymous, explained when questioned about the legal rights of parents to remain in contact with their own biological children. "Automatically, they don't have any right automatically, but they have an automatic right to apply for rights"[51]

The Family Court of Australia agreed with that legal opinion, when in the leading case on this matter, Brown and Peterson (1992), the judges said: "This Court has long laid to rest any notion that a parent

---

50 "Sanctioned by the State", Family Briefing, 2015
51 Family Briefing – "Children of the State (MP3) Part 1"

has a right to access." The court spelled out that it may decide to grant access, but "until such order is made no right of access exists".

This means, since no presumptive legal right exists for parents to parent their own children, the only option parents have to seek the legal protection of their biological children is to either commence expensive legal proceedings to beg for the right to do so, or accept the forced abandonment of their children.

Coupled with the fact that court orders are not enforced by family courts, seeking non-existent rights and justice in our family courts has become an expensive exercise in futility and a perfect storm for rampant child removals.

The fact that eight out of 10 children lose the protection of their family as a result, has been recorded in recurring ABS family characteristics surveys.

And as John Stapleton, a veteran journalist and co-founder of the world's longest running father's radio show, *Dads on the Air*, wrote in *Chaos at the Crossroads: Family Law Reform in Australia*:

> Successive governments from both left and right have failed to listen to their constituents and respond to their concerns. Even when enacting legislative reforms, these same governments left their enforcement in the hands of institutions notoriously resistant to change. They allowed or encouraged fashionable ideology, institutional inertia and bureaucracy to triumph over common sense. Common decency was lost long ago.
>
> Overly legalistic, enormously bureaucratic, secretive, unaccountable and ideologically based, defying community

norms of morality and propriety, the Family Court soon became one of the country's most hated institutions. The court has also ordered litigants not to contact the United Nations with their concerns, not to publicise the injustices of their cases in any way and not to take their children to a doctor or raise welfare concerns.

In terms of human suffering, the public has already paid dearly for the failure to reform outdated, badly administered and inappropriate institutions dealing with family breakdown and for the failure of governments to take seriously the voices of the men and women most directly affected by them. The country's failure to reform family law and child support is ultimately a failure of democracy itself. As it stands, the lawyers, liars, bureaucrats and social engineers have won the day.[52]

Australian Professor John Hirst also argued in 2005 that the same standards we apply to intact families should apply to separated families and points out that the court has rejected that idea and insists that there is no presumptive right for a parent to see a child. "The court will decide in its judgment whether it is in the best interest of the child for the parents to see them".

There is great danger in elevating one purpose as the only purpose to be pursued. This is the totalitarian impulse. We see its evils clearly in the extreme cases when the purpose was the racial purity of the German people or the defence of the proletarian revolution in Russia. But it should be

---

52 Stapleton, John. *Chaos at the Crossroads: Family Law Reform in Australia*. A Sense of Place Publishing, 2013.

remembered that the people who performed horrible deeds for those causes thought they were good causes. We all think the defence of children is a good cause, but we cannot pursue this as a purpose in whose name anything can be excused.[53]

It should be noted that courts only interpret and apply the laws, they do not make them. Bad laws nevertheless produce bad outcomes and it is the legislation that clearly confirms there is no presumptive legal right for either a parent or a child to remain in any type of protective contact with each other following parental separation.

It is chilling to find that no parent or child has a presumptive legal right to the protection of their biological family. That once ensnared in the web of child-removal networks it becomes virtually impossible for children to escape the severing of important kinship bonds or access the physical and emotional protection that they provide.

Unfortunately, the relentless focus by many reform campaigners and social justice advocates on shared parenting and the abolition of Family Courts in order to stop child removals is misguided and shows there is an absence of understanding of the root cause of policy failure and what the big picture presents. It is akin to abolitionist calling for an end to slavery and focusing all their energies on the behaviour of slave owners, slave auctioneers or those captaining the slave ships.

It was the legislation that legitimised the enslavement of one group of humans by another that was the root cause of the problem then, and it is the legislation that is legitimising the unfettered mass removal

---

53 Hirst, John, "Kangaroo Court: Family Law in Australia", *Quarterly Essay*, Issue 17, 2005

of millions of children from their families that is the root cause of the problem now.

Children of the State has attempted to move the argument beyond the previous excellent attempts by numerous authors and critics to expose the fundamental flaws in systems that have increasingly appropriated the control of people's lives into their own ambit. This is achieved by hiding behind "the best interest of the child" criterion, which in all too many cases may as well be a generic term for: "I have no idea what I'm talking about, but it sounds good."

We have also tried to move beyond traditional gender-based arguments over men's rights or women's rights, to avoid the quagmire of conflicting ideologies involved in the endless well of pain that is family law. Any law that does more harm than good is obviously not fit for purpose, yet family and child-protection laws, which demonstrably fail to protect those mostly in need of protection, have continued to flourish under the stewardship of successive national and state governments, irrespective of their political persuasions.

Finally, we were able to establish with some certainty: a) the number of people negatively impacted by the large-scale removal of millions of children from the protection of their families worldwide, and b) the immense scale of the crippling social and economic costs forced upon the community that have come as a result.

The astonishing levels of dysfunction, the poor outcomes and the extremely high levels of dissatisfaction inherent in the overlapping jurisdictions of children, family and criminal courts, which are protected so ably by protection orders, secrecy provisions, the utter cowardice and complicity of politicians, and numerous taxpayer-funded lobby groups sprouting bigoted gender ideologies, have been allowed to take the system hostage.

Many billions of dollars have been spent on industries promoting the best interests of the child, with not a shred of evidence that the policies and procedures in place actually work.

Those who attempt to debate the subject are almost invariably howled down by their taxpayer-funded critics. But in the end, it is our failure to be vigilant that has prevented us from moving forward.

Moreover, it is the collective failure of courage to stand up for freedom of expression and our reluctance to demand the right to engage in a civilised debate on a level playing field that have led to the present dire situation.

A legal fiction masquerading as a legal principle is the "Best Interest of the Child" mantra. Used ad nauseam, this phrase makes a mockery of the idea that the rule of law should govern a nation, as opposed to being governed by the arbitrary decisions of individual government officials.

There is a well-recognised phenomenon where someone initially alleges something about another person and it gets repeated and repeated, quoted by various experts and firmed up across multiple documents and court hearings. Fiction becomes fact, certainly when left in the hands of lawyers. This is the effect of an unsubstantiated allegation or record of suspicion – it can often be revived again and again and is very damaging for a disempowered parent who has done nothing wrong, other than express an inherent wish to remain in their child's life in order to protect him or her from harm.

Not well understood by most, but celebrated by predatory system functionaries, is the sad reality that within the jurisdiction of family and child-protection laws, normal, well-adjusted human beings are behaving exactly the way an emotionally charged adversarial system of justice would expect them to behave. It is a system set up to ensnare as many people as possible, with little or no concern for the disastrous consequences this social engineering experiment is inflicting with the forced separating of families and children.

Who is prepared to go to court and spend the whole of their life savings to ensure their child is protected from harm? The answer lies in the fact that, with very few exceptions, it is in our human DNA to want to protect our biological offspring from harm at any cost. Therefore, the answer is a resounding "every one of us".

After more than 40 years, however, most people no longer have faith in a system of justice where the rule of law is an illusion and checks and balances are ignored or do not exist. Far from abandoning their children, the vast majority either refuse to waste their children's inheritance fighting for rights they do not have, or they lack the required skills and economic resources to mount a case as a self-representing litigant, or they have already been removed from their children's lives due to being falsely accused of family violence, or face the threat thereof should they initiate proceedings.

The end result is that a massive 95 per cent of families are forced to negotiate and settle their case under duress, in the shadow of a set of legal rules that in reality resemble the rule of the jungle. For the vast majority of families, the relationship with their children is severely compromised. Many children and parents never recover, struggling to survive from one day to the next.

This is in stark contrast to the fashionable establishment contention that most people resolve their separations in a peaceful and amicable manner and arrive at a mutually agreeable outcome. Without the presence of any academic research ever being produced anywhere in the world in support of such a contention, the myth nevertheless has grown legs and is deviously used by those who benefit financially from artful propaganda.

Perhaps unsurprisingly, very little information is available on the social and economic outcomes and the impact they have on the whole of community. At a national level, investigative data analysis in this sensitive area is even more difficult to find. With the notable exception of Australia, every nation state has so far neglected to regularly gather the comprehensive national information necessary that would allow its citizens to inform and alert their elected political leadership to the abject failure of their policies.

After five years of intense scrutiny of government documents, meticulous data analysis and combing through many hours of audio and video evidence, Family Briefing was finally able to join all the dots. By so doing, we are now able to expose a global family and child-protection catastrophe, which is destroying the lives of millions, costing billions and ignores alternatives. The "who, what, where, when, why and how" government initiated family destruction has been allowed to continue uninterrupted for the past 40 years, is now well-documented in this book. It clearly shows how global nation states have been allowed to crush the life out of protective family relationships and in so doing remove generations of children from the protection of their biological families at will. It is hoped that with this new information, *Children of the State* will contribute to a much needed counter narrative so urgently required to challenge and stem the flow of misinformation that is underpinning the well-oiled propaganda machine of the currently fashionable, enabling ruling elite.

It is also a sad reality that some of the world's most powerful intellects have wrestled with the very same problems as presented in this book. They have documented in great detail the ensnaring power of the state, the misguided and ideologically driven nature of dysfunctional systems, and the terrible consequences for men, women, children and extended families.

Many warnings have been issued as to the totalitarian nature of these systems, the hoodwinking of the public, the stifling of debate and the marginalisation and discrediting of those who dare to speak out against them.

Most reformers, no matter how highly motivated and well intentioned however, give up in the face of a deluge of government-funded propaganda emanating from numerous agencies. Over time, they burn out. Completely disillusioned, they feel personally diminished and ultimately distrustful and disengaged from a society and a democracy they once, naively, believed worked for the benefit of the citizenry.

These courageous, outspoken souls include men, women and children, most of whom share a dreadful life experience no one had prepared them for.

One of the most analytical of these exponents has been Professor Stephen Baskerville, whose *Taken into Custody* exposed what he argued was the greatest and most destructive civil rights abuse in America.

He reasoned that family courts and Soviet-style bureaucracies have trampled basic civil liberties, entering homes uninvited and taking away people's children at will, then throwing the parents in jail without any form of due process, much less a trial.

> "No parent, no child, no family in America is safe" he argues. "The legal industry does not want you to hear this story." He further affirms: "Bar associations, and social work bureaucracies have colluded to suppress this information. Even pro-family groups and civil libertarians look the other way. Yet it is a reality for tens of millions of Americans who are our neighbours.[54]

Another outspoken critic of contemporary family and child-protection laws is Stephen Krasner, who has extensive experience in the area of law, politics, community activism and complex research and analysis.

He has recently written a series of articles on the issue titled "A Broken System" for the *Huffington Post*.

He asserts: "Non-custodial parents have now become the mothers or fathers unwillingly offered up as an integral part of the 'supply' to the 'demands' of the multibillion dollars a year global Family Law industry. Think of it like a gift that keeps on giving in many scenarios when viewed through the lenses of the family court apparatuses at play."

> The answer is complex in explanation – yet simple to describe with one word in far too many situations of this nature – *money!* … Following the money takes you on a convoluted path of trickle down funding, incentivised

---

[54] Baskerville, op. cit. 2007

motives, political distributions, allotments buried in legislative meeting minutes and contracts all forming one very tangled web within the lucrative industry of Family Law … It leaves a wake of devastated lives, denied liberties and seized property that put many in a place where weathering such conditions becomes a lifestyle set in constant survival mode … Most alarming is not the uniqueness of each case, but rather the shared commonalities and level of frequency, abuses in this area of law take place.[55]

In recent times, the world has seen the political and institutional leadership of many countries line up to apologise for the negligence of their predecessors to fulfil their moral and legal obligations to protect and take care of their nations' children. There were numerous powerful speeches that brought many to tears as they listened to the deep felt emotional outpourings of regret and sorrow and everyone was heartened by their promises to never, ever allow such failings to occur again.

But, their inability to recognise their government's own participation in the very same child-protection policy failures as those they were accusing their predecessors of and were so passionately apologising for reflects badly on the lack of empathy and quality of their political judgements and leadership.

In October 2017, the Australian Prime Minister Malcolm Turnbull stood up in our national Parliament and offering condolences said: "As parents, our worst dread is the loss of a child". The then-opposition leader, Bill Shorten, chimed in and added: "Losing a child is

---

55 Krasner, Stephen. A collection of quotes from: "A Broken System", *Huffington Post*, 2017.

every parent's nightmare. It is, as Shakespeare once said, a grief that fills the room."[56]

Their condolences however, should be measured against their do-nothing attitude in relation to Australian-Government-sponsored child-removal policies.

On any given day, an estimated 830,000 Australian minor children, are denied vital family protection, while 352,000 Australian parents are denied the opportunity to protect their biological children. Not to mention the millions of extended family members likewise denied the opportunity to protect their biological family from harm.

The shedding of political crocodile tears, therefore, is a poor hypocritical substitute for decisive humanitarian action to protect their fellow citizens from government-perpetrated maltreatment!

---

56 Bickers, Claire, "Labor MP Linda Burney's Son Found Dead", *News.com.au*, 25 Oct., 2017. Accessed here: http://www.news.com.au/national/politics/labor-mp-linda-burneys-son-found-dead/news-story/aae0a2ef18188329f06943b888467965

Nine

The Domestic Violence Phenomena

DONALD TRUMP didn't win an unwinnable election; Hillary Clinton lost an unlosable one. Some of the Washington swamp was certainly drained, but one malodorous sludge was simply replaced by another.

Did a dumbfounded political leadership really learn anything?

With breathtaking ignorance, Clinton failed to realise the bigotry of her radical gender ideology, when she subsequently made sweeping gender divisive statements about the "presence of endemic sexism and misogyny". Sanctimoniously suggesting that anybody who tries to disagree with her and claim otherwise was either "blind or disingenuous".[57]

She admitted that Democrats have had a problem with white voters including white women for a long time, but failed to realise that by cherry-picking a few high-profile male predators in order to stereotype the whole of the American male population as sexists and misogynists was turning an increasing number of women away from politics.

---

57 Ferguson, Sarah, "Hillary Clinton: The Interview", *Four Corners*, ABC News, 16 Oct. 2017. Accessed here: http://www.abc.net.au/4corners/hillary-clinton:-the-interview/9055256, and includes transcript.

Millions of women have experienced first-hand the social and economic consequences of the systemic demonising of their fathers, grandfathers, sons, brothers and male partners, that triggered their separation from their children.

For many decades, social scientists, journalists and policymakers, have focused on creating gender-divisive policies that have done nothing except exacerbate the problem of large-scale child removals.

Ignored is the fact that in today's world, the consequences of parenting and relationship breakdown are one of the central problems faced by many societies. At the heart of one of the greatest social injustices of all time is the way such breakdowns are managed by contemporary governments. A contentious family and child-protection bureaucracy has been created, which is now ineradicably entrenched at the very core of massive discontent throughout our communities.

It is a fact of life that there will always be a percentage of relationships that fail and that some interpersonal violence and abuse will always be an unfortunate part of the human condition. This does not mean violence and abuse should ever be tolerated, far from it. But instead, the present situation, where governments have deliberately created gendered moral panic to justify extensive state interference in private lives, clearly demands common sense debate. Surely all victims need to be protected by a set of community safety standards that provide equal protection for all.

Instead, it is the powerful domestic-violence sector governments have created that is blocking the path out of the morass contemporary society finds itself in. Perfectly decent, hard-working citizens find themselves facing false or highly exaggerated and inflammatory allegations, leading to disempowerment, ridicule, and marginalisation. With a battery of lawyers and courts, it is persecution by process.

Much of the debate is driven by radical gender theory, which creates more problems than it solves. Replacing one group of pathological child removers with another serves no one. As we were to learn later, these inhumane practices date back hundreds of years and are repeated in different formulae within each generation.

The simple lack of studies undertaken to indicate the effectiveness or otherwise of highly expensive campaigns speaks to a bureaucracy that cannot stand the light. The billions of dollars spent on domestic violence has not led to resolution of the problem, but to ever more extreme claims of an "epidemic", requiring, of course, ever more funds.

The path towards sound policy development should not be so difficult. But somehow we never seem to learn from history. Each generation is compelled to go through the same painful processes. If it was easy to solve major social justice policy failures, we would simply be able to go back to previous works and learn from the mistakes of our forebears. But we don't. The same culture wars are fought by each new generation. Different lines are used, different titles are invented and new methods are devised to achieve the same goals, but the same endgame is acquired at the expense of a calamitous price for children. Each generation has its own heroes and villains, championed and vilified by the herd. Every mistake we make is made over and over again.

Unless we confront the child-removal issues of our generation with factual evidence and until we are able to rouse the silent majority and draw attention to the daily dangers that they and their families face, further generations of vulnerable children will continue to suffer.

Without a new approach founded on sound research, there will continue to be further desperate and doomed attempts at reform and social outcomes, while the electorate will have no alternative but to experience the same dreadful consequences.

As we repeat these things in the 21st Century, they simply have different labels. They are hidden behind the hysterical rhetoric of the mostly populist, ideology-driven agendas of those locked into unrealistic but extremely dangerous ideas.

One of those extremely dangerous ideas came to fruition in Australia in late 2005, when the Victorian state government legislated for a law that would accommodate women taking the law into their own hands. It was created to make it easier for them to be excused for murdering their male partner by being able to claim their acts were the end result of domestic violence.

It was a homicide law intended to enable women to blame their dead victims provided they were male. But committing lethal violence with an intention to kill is murder and the operation of defensive homicide laws in Victoria unjustly blurred the distinction between murder and less culpable forms of homicide.

Incredibly, the Victorian government created a legal defence mechanism intended to favour the murder of one gender only. It was the stuff of nightmares for the mothers of sons, but a win for the agenda of radical gender ideologues.

It ignored the long-held legal and community standard that, as a fundamental principle of the criminal justice system, all people should be equal before the law and not treated in a discriminatory manner. Civilised societies no longer accept that laws should be targeted at, or be tailored to specifically fit one gender or colour at the expense of the other.

The defensive homicide law was abolished however, only after it was found men were also using it to escape murder convictions and shamefully not because of its intent to favour one gender over the other.

The Victorian Department of Justice released a consultation paper, which proposed to abolish the controversial offence of defensive homicide after its more than seven years in operation. Exposing departmental gender bigotry, the consultation paper found that "there is no clear evidence that defensive homicide is working in the way intended to support women who kill in response to family violence. Further, there is some evidence to suggest that its existence may be counter-productive."[58]

Gender bigotry is well and truly on the march and its critics gagged. Blinded by self-righteousness, its exponents are oblivious to the irreparable damage they are inflicting on their children, the nation's next generation.

In today's world, global regressive left activists claim to be fighting against "fascism" or "the extreme right". Ironically, these are the very same people who repeatedly resort to classic 1930s fascist tactics such as wrecking the public meetings of their opponents, and see nothing wrong with harassing or attacking attendees. If they are unable to prevent an opponent's meeting taking place by threatening or fright-

---

58 State Government Victoria, Department of Justice, "Defensive Homicide: Proposals for Legislative Reform: Consultation Paper", p. 26. Published by Criminal Law Review, Sept. 2013. Full text available here: https://assets.justice.vic.gov.au/justice/resources/f9d7181e-5bef-47b6-814b-183eeb8d8be5/defensivehomicideconsultation-paper2013.pdf

ening the venue operators, they will turn up at meetings not to challenge or debate an issue, but with the sole purpose of disrupting, silencing and shutting their opponents down.

For them, the means justifies the end and their actions are non-negotiable. The fact that much available evidence suggest major harm is being perpetrated against the very societal group they zealously claim to want to protect, cannot be spoken about.

The ferociousness of McCarthyism or the Salem witch trials can be seen in the lynch-mob mentality of the domestic-violence debate. Either you agree uncritically to the massive expansion of the state that domestic violence legislation enables, or you are a misogynistic apologist for the patriarchy. The laws are based on a few extreme cases and then generalised to the broader public.

The authorities know perfectly well that the legislation is frequently misused by vindictive partners attempting to gain leverage in child-custody cases, that it encourages false accusations, and that it causes these ideologically and loosely drafted laws to be hated by many of those in the police services forced to administer them.

Some social commentators, when confronted with evidence that does not fit their narrative or ideology, will dismiss the challenge by claiming not enough research is available to provide a clear picture and then go on to present misinformation and half-truths as fact.

* * *

Flying under the radar and completely overlooked, has been the extent to which domestic violence legislation is implicated in the creation of contemporary child-removal policies. The relocation of children is either interrelated with the redistribution of wealth or a power play for dominance.

Almost all domestic violence accusations are either made leading up to, during, or shortly after parental separation, in order to gain a legal advantage and are now an integral part of the family and child-protection legal system.

That society needs to be protected from violent and abusive members of the human family is not in question, since common sense alone dictates that for a healthy society to flourish it has to function in a safe and nourishing environment. There should be no support at all for those who arbitrarily abuse the weak. But when a societal safety net against violence and abuse is created that serves to protect only a privileged section of society and stereotypes everyone else as a potential perpetrator of violence from birth, other more sinister and dangerous philosophies and objectives are at play that fly in the face of balance, justice and equality.

The bar is now set so low in family/domestic violence law, that each and every citizen can now be considered both an abuser and a victim. In fact, using the current definition of domestic violence and abuse, we have all been raised in dysfunctional, abusive homes. We can all now be considered as victims of abuse and every one of our parents and grandparents now classified as violent and abusive perpetrators of domestic violence.

But there is an unrecognised and extremely dangerous method in the madness, since setting the bar this low provides governments the legal authority to remove most children from their families and redistribute them as they see fit.

Accordingly, children have never had more to fear from their governments as they do now in the 21st Century. In the heat of the moment, parents in the process of dealing with the painful stress of relationship breakdown are far too often tempted to make use of this baited trap set for them by their governments.

They do not realise that by falling victim to the temptation to make a claim of domestic violence against their ex-partner, often encouraged by their lawyers, they are placing their children in immediate danger of being targeted for future removal from their care.

By making a domestic violence claim, irrespective of whether it is genuine or false, their children are automatically sucked into the system and considered as vulnerable victims and placed on a watch list.

Government agencies and for-profit corporations are waiting in the wings for these children, while the populist self-interest focus of our elected political representatives cause them to continue to turn a blind eye to what subsequently happens to these children.

In today's frenetic character-assassinating climate, to be born a male or non-white child, means you can be targeted and marked for life as inherently inferior and potentially threatening, within dominant white population groups.

Proudly promoted as serving to protect society from harmful actions inflicted by dangerous males or non-whites, current domestic violence legislation has expanded and become society's own worst nightmare. It has become a vehicle for the lawful stereotyping and marginalising of half of our civilian population. Once so stereotyped and marked as a potential threat, the dominant population group is provided with the legal tenure to claim ownership of and redistribute the children and economic resources of those legally disempowered.

The resulting fires of community discontent, fuelled by the fears and hatred of those burned by systemic persecution at the hands of such a system, are ignored by governments at their own peril. They are creating a large, embittered, disenfranchised group which in the end does the broader society no good at all.

Families and children dispossessed of the protection of their families as a result of governments ignoring their warnings against the disastrous consequences of their destructive policies, will not be easily forgiving of those who abused the trust placed in them.

Most child removals are initiated by either a self-absorbed dysfunctional parent, a vexatious ex-partner, or an overzealous bureaucrat and take place in the shadow of the law. While at the same time and, contrary to the popular myth promulgated by industry ideologues, most maligned parents who end up living without their biological children are not associated with voluntary abandonment of their children at all. Without any legal right to protect their own biological children and set upon if they dare to object, they are left with no other choice.

It is simply not in the human DNA of either mothers or fathers to abandon their offspring willingly. There is an inherent instinct within all parents to protect their children from any harm they may face. But right throughout history, governments have found many ingenious ways, covertly and overtly, to circumvent these powerful human qualities and remove many generations of children from the protection of their family.

The scorched-earth policies of the domestic-violence sector acting with the zealotry of McCarthyism on steroids, is one of those manipulators of the human spirit and is now proving to be every mother's worst nightmare.

Watching on in horror, mothers and grandmothers around the globe are witnessing every one of their sons and grandsons being portrayed and labelled as potential domestic violence perpetrators even from a tender age.

Being negatively targeted and collectively labelled as impending abusers throughout their school years, many boys are struggling with their inherent male instinct to protect girls from harm.

Throughout human history, men and boys have always been looked upon as protectors, and many millions have sacrificed their lives in distant wars, in the belief it was their fundamental duty to prevent harm coming to the women and children in their communities. It was what society expected them to do and they did so willingly.

An avalanche of negative propaganda, however, now portrays all males as a dangerous species to be feared by society and who need to be removed from any close association with women and children, creating the perfect conditions for the child-removal sector.

As their sons attain adulthood and form relationships, mothers note how they continue to be singled out for special attention because of their gender and how they are further labelled as violent abusers not worthy of maintaining relationships with their own biological children.

Concerned mothers are absolutely horrified at subsequently seeing their sons stripped of their families, possessions and humanity, on account of a flimsy fabricated allegation of violence or abuse, concocted with absolute impunity by a vindictive ex-partner. Biological parents and grandparents likewise find themselves persecuted by being denied access to, and the protection of, their grandchildren.

In Australia, grandmother groups have been at the forefront of every family law enquiry and are currently the driving force behind the calls for the return of Indigenous children to their culture and families.

An ideologically divisive industry that targets and considers only people of one gender or colour as perpetrators is a bigoted industry by any definition and should have no place in contemporary society. The fact that the domestic violence industry does and is costing Australian taxpayers an estimated $22 billion per annum[59] is disgraceful and will remain a blot on our country's perception of justice and fairness.

Androphobia[60] (an irrational, misplaced fear of men) is being propagated, exploited and turned into a fear-mongering industry designed to single out just one gender and in so doing, progressively turn the population against all men. It is used to create public hysteria and generate extensive government funding.

Girls from a tender age are now commonly taught to stay away from the opposite sex and this fear continues to be ingrained during their childhood. Prejudiced, paranoid or obsessed caregivers, parents or grandparents can also be responsible for instilling such fear in young minds. Constant paranoid warnings such as, "stay away from strange

---

59 Report prepared for the Department of Social Services by KPMG: "The Cost of Violence Against Women and their Children in Australia", May, 2016. Accessed here: https://www.dss.gov.au/sites/default/files/documents/08_2016/the_cost_of_violence_against_women_and_their_children_in_australia_-_summary_report_may_2016.pdf

60 Irrational, abnormal fear of men; an aversion towards the male sex.

men, do not drive in a car with a man" or "do not sit next to a man", can lead to reprogramming of the brain and turn perfectly normal kids into speciously induced androphobes.

TV shows, movies, and news reports of rape, kidnapping, or murder, can also lead to such irrational fear of men.

Fear however, has progressively morphed into hatred.

This can be seen in the ceaseless marketing campaigns funded by the domestic-violence sector, which is happy to present a repetitive and unrealistic portrayal of all men and boys as violent abusive bullies, who happily bully and bash defenceless women and children.

For many years now successive governments of all persuasions have encouraged and enthusiastically funded the ideological thrashing of half of their national population base, in the misguided belief that the female vote would be lost if they were to do otherwise.

This extremely harmful and divisive practice has gone on to destroy the lives of millions of men, women and children, because of a gender prejudice that stereotypes all males as bad and all females as beyond reproach.

The fact that every male has a mother and grandmother, and that many have sisters, wives and daughters who watch their partners, sons, brothers and fathers pilloried and stereotyped as violent abusers because of their gender and who are horrified at the dreadful consequences they witness does not seem to concern our elected representatives. Their votes apparently do not count, and the numerous votes of all these "dreadful" males are also rendered inert.

But the world is changing. Those who have gotten away for many years with tearing apart valuable kinship bonds and denied millions of children the protection of their families for political, ideological, personal or economic advantage, are being called out.

In many countries, voters are turning away from the major parties because of their elitist attitudes and sense of entitlement. New alternatives have become available. The old guard are being challenged and cast aside in increasing numbers.

Having their pleas for equality and social justice ignored for many years, the electorate are discovering new political candidates who are prepared to listen to their concerns and are willing to stand up and challenge the state's abuse of their constituents.

In Australia alone, many men and the women who love them, have now turned to candidates such as Senators Pauline Hanson, Jacqui Lambie, John Madigan, Derryn Hinch and David Leyonhjelm, political figures who have at least shown a willingness to call for a major enquiry into the consequences of federal family and child-protection policies and practices. This is unsurprising, since at the same time, the major parties appear to be single-mindedly intent on continuing to throw more taxpayer dollars at their failed policies. All this in the vain hope that their dereliction of duty and failure to act appropriately to protect the nation's children and their families would continue to remain concealed from the public.

In today's world, to be labelled a homophobe, Islamophobe or xenophobe, immediately discounts your contribution to many important debates. A tactic used to silence opponents, these are the most common labels given to anyone who dares to provide an alternative view to that relentlessly promoted by the establishment or by those with the most funding or political influence. Irrespective of how prejudiced, hateful or bigoted a popular public perception might be, if you are referred to as a "…phobe", you are ostracised and eliminated from the debate on the grounds your position is considered inferior to the mainstream perspective. It is a popular label put on those that the establishment wish to remove from relevance.

Not so for those promoting and working in the domestic violence sector, however. Considered untouchable, they are free to distribute misinformation; safe in the knowledge that the accuracy of their assertions will never be seriously challenged. These are luxuries not afforded those who dare to challenge the sector and who are generally reduced to the status of "patriarchal", "misogynistic" or "xenophobic".

The result is that an Australian government-funded industry, which is annually costing taxpayers $22 billion dollars, has been allowed to remain untouchable, casting half of the Australian population as violent patriarchal bullies and the other half as brutalised shrinking violets. The intellectual underpinnings may be wobbly at best, but this publicly funded sector operates in a bubble, completely free from fear of being challenged.

The promotion of an absurd one-eyed view of the world such as that promoted by the current family-violence sector, belongs to that of the mythical Greek Cyclopes: who see with only one eye, in only one dimension and only half of reality. Such people stereotype the male by the actions of a minority, define the exceptions as the rule, ignore the majority, and ignore too, the minority of female villains. Supposedly, this presents a cleaner, clearer picture. Ignored is the fact that while many murderers are male, most males are not murderers and that many females are murderers too, but again not all females are murderers.

The result of our own research certainly suggests, the one-sided debate in support of current domestic violence policy is infinitely less about reality than about politics. It is immeasurably more about maintaining government-funded cash flows than protecting people from harm.

In fact, the bar that defines domestic violence is now set so low that no one is able to slip under it. The flimsiest of allegations, such as a raised voice, a stare, giving someone the silent treatment or even a "perceived" fear of someone during their lifetime, enables every man, woman and child to be defined as both, an abusive perpetrator or a helpless victim. Any disagreement between parents automatically defines children as victims of abuse and renders them vulnerable to the little known supremacy of state guardianship powers.

Meanwhile, quite incredulously, a number of criminal actions, which serve to lower the protective safety shield for children and increase their exposure to abuse – such as parental kidnapping, perjury, contempt of court, or perverting the course of justice – are not considered abusive actions against families or children.

That the inclusion of such criminal actions to the definition of family violence and abuse would radically alter national statistical outcomes, especially in relation to the gender and relationship of domestic violence perpetrators to their victims, is not lost on those calling for a drastic overhaul of the sector.

But placing an obstacle between a bucket load of government money and a power-hungry sector blinded by self-interest, presents a formidable challenge.

In the 21st Century, a hysterical, unproven allegation is all that is required to separate children from a biological parent. That parent is subsequently relieved of their assets and has their reputation and employment opportunities destroyed. In many cases, this treatment is the primary catalyst for a host of induced physical and mental health problems.

No supporting evidence is required and either a genuine or fabricated allegation is enough to achieve the required result of separating children from parents. If in due course the allegation is found to be fabricated, the perjuring accuser will be punished with the equivalent of a slap on the wrist at best, depending on the generosity of the judiciary.

The main objective will have been achieved, however, with the time a child is kept away from a falsely accused parent being used to manipulate and radicalise the child to hate their absent parent, and by inducing what has been referred to as the "Independent Thinker Phenomenon".[61]

Subsequently, the judiciary are prone to leave the children in the care of such dysfunctional, perjuring parent and in the interest of judicial expediency, claim that such ruling is in the "best interest of the child".

Despite the fact that most allegations of violence and abuse are initi-

---

[61] Bone, J. Michael, *"Independent Thinker Phenomenon"*, YouTube, 27 February, 2009. (J. Michael Bone, PhD. is a consultant for cases involving "Parental Alienation" and has spent more than 25 years working in the area of high-conflict divorce as a therapist, expert witness, mediator, evaluator and consultant. He is co-founder of the US National Association of Parental Alienation Specialists. The phenomenon "refers to the consistent behaviour seen in alienated children where they claim that their resistance to seeing an 'unfavoured' or targeted parent derives from their own independent thought and is not the result of the other parent's influence". Bone (2017), *The Eight Symptoms of Parental Alienation: Independent Thinker Phenomenon*, https://www.linkedin.com/pulse/eight-symptoms-parental-alienation-independent-j-michael-bone-phd

ated by women against men, with the domestic violence bar set so low, men are also able to successfully initiate allegations of abuse and increasingly do so.

As was seen with the defensive homicide laws in Victoria, once men realise the only guaranteed way to maintain contact with their children is to overcome their natural instincts and likewise begin to engage in making pre-emptive false claims of violence or abuse, bigoted laws will be repealed.

In the meantime, the most unfortunate result for children is that currently, either one of their parents is able to launch a pre-emptive first strike and eliminate the other parent from the children's life and, by so doing, place them on a child-removal watch list. Once alone with the children, any vindictive parent is able to initiate the mind-altering radicalisation process.

There is also a tendency to muddy the waters when presenting the data on domestic violence, such as with the blurring of the distinction between allegations and substantiated outcomes. While there is an obvious marked difference, often the two are presented to appear as one set of "substantiated" allegations of violence and abuse. Such blurring of the facts is rarely questioned by policymakers or the media and goes straight through to the keeper. Nevertheless, it is very successful in distorting public perceptions.

Fuelling the failure of rational debate is their often gender-divisive nature further sanctioned by policies created by successive ham-fisted governments.

For many decades these have served to divide and weaken any credible opposition and encouraged the use of misleading and questionable data to formulate substandard policy development.

Whoever genuinely believes in equality does not criticise authentic feminism or the notion of gender equality. Most people accept that in today's more enlightened world, it is unacceptable and counterproductive to demand a return to a patriarchal society. The supremacy of patriarchy has shown it was far from in "the best interest of children" to have one parent in total control of their life, since many children's lives were destroyed by the often dysfunctional behaviour of that controlling, dominant parent. The sense of superiority and entitlement that was habitually associated with such unfettered control of a family's children was the source of much adverse reaction and in many cases proved extremely detrimental to the children's long-term well-being.

Yet, once again, we see a repeat of the worst characteristics of the human psyche being displayed in the quest for contemporary gender superiority. With the abandonment of the notion of patriarchal superiority began the quest for superiority entitlements as witnessed by the subsequent matriarchal gender demands, couched in a thinly veiled pursuit for equality.

Prepared to sacrifice the children of relationships on the altar of ideology in order to gain the superior bargaining position, has, since the 1970s, seen more than 80 per cent of biological children from parents whose relationship broke down ending up in the primary care of their biological mothers with little or no contact with their absent biological fathers.[62] No longer able to protect their biological offspring from harm, a host of disabling situations have emerged for both the children and their forcibly absent biological family members.

---

62 ABS, "Family Characteristics 2009-10, Australia", Paper 4442.0. Accessed here: http://www.abs.gov.au/AUSSTATS/abs@.nsf/DetailsPage/4442.02009-10?OpenDocument

While all men are now marginalised and stereotyped as a potential danger to their children and family, those who dare to speak out against the blanket, negative demonization of men and who call for true gender equality are now ridiculed and dismissed as misogynists.

The well-oiled taxpayer-funded propaganda machine of the domestic-violence sector is a powerful political lobby group that has struck pay dirt with an ongoing campaign to criticise and generate the fear of men in our communities. The result serves to separate children from the protection of their families and guarantees a government-funded cash flow to finance ideological hate campaigns against men.

Anyone who dares to question this sector for even the slightest irregularity in their often outlandish claims are immediately attacked for the audacity to criticise or question them, or worse still, dare to call them to account. Off-limits to criticism, a movement has developed that has been given free rein to perpetrate hate speech in order to generate government funding.

Safe in the knowledge that they will not be challenged, this sector has claimed legal ownership of children by stealth. What began as a reasonable and rational campaign to prevent domestic violence or decrease interpersonal violence, soon morphed into a campaign to prevent violence against women and, once so established, into a hysterical crusade to prevent violence against "Women and Their Children". While no legal ownership of children exists in any democracy for parents to make that claim, Australian Prime Minister Malcolm Turnbull nevertheless proudly displayed the deliberately deceptive claim of ownership in bold letters on the homepage of his prime ministerial taxpayer-funded blog.

Due to most people being unaware of the demonstrable falseness of the claim, it can now be found in much of the literature in support of the domestic-violence sector.

We wondered at the lack of critical media vigilance or questioning evaluation, and were perplexed by the failure to fact check, challenge, and alert the public to an obvious sleight of hand by a powerful ideological lobby group. Such failure in public scrutiny has provided much oxygen to misinformation being used to support the objectives of those engaged in the redistribution of children for profit and the resulting community fragmentation into a collection of self-interest groups.

* * *

The vast majority of rational, well-balanced mothers on the other hand, those who love the men and children in their lives and do not have fear or hatred in their heart or share the lynch-mob mentality and twisted views of a currently fashionable minority of their sisters, now look at their baby boys and are afraid of what awaits them as they mature into men and fathers.

They are ardently against all violence and abuse, but do not support dishonest campaigns that intentionally promote violence and abuse as only being perpetrated by one gender. These women believe in a balanced approach, instead of the witch-hunts singling out their loved ones. Over recent times these mothers have been bombarded by television advertising and one-eyed or misinformed social commentators, depicting all of their partners, brothers, fathers and male children as all bad and all women and girls as all good. They are deeply concerned for their men, and, since the major political parties show no interest in the concerns they have for their loved ones, have started voting with their feet.

Despite their demise, and acting like lemmings going over the cliff, most voters up until recently have shown a willingness to stick with the donkey vote and keep electing old-guard politicians representing do-nothing parties.

On behalf of antiquated parties espousing regressive politics, these fence-sitting relics have shown no interest in their concerns and ignored their pleas for help. Much talk of progressive, innovative policies, but very little action.

Such political apathy breeds discontent, but some small signs of changing attitudes are beginning to emerge, giving hope that eventually common sense will prevail and in due course lead to much needed change.

Future generations of children depend on our generosity of spirit and willingness to fight for the abolition of unjustified child removals, which will see them relieved from having to travel down the same rocky road as today's children. It is incumbent upon those with vision, therefore, to ensure the next generation of children does not have to endure the spectacle of the prejudiced public demonising of *their* parents.

The power and influence enjoyed by prominent lobby groups, such as the domestic-violence sector however, will be extremely difficult to curb.

Indications are that they are certainly not going to relinquish their lucrative funding source and all-powerful position of dominance without a fight.

When Queensland Premier Annastacia Palaszczuk made headlines by calling for media campaigns against domestic violence to include male victims, her comment was met by a barrage of complaints from domestic-violence services, warning her not to recognise male victims at the expense of women.[63]

It may well be, nevertheless, that those times are beginning to change. Witness the rise of independents in most western democracies and their influence within an increasing number of minority governments requiring their support. These politicians present a refreshing change outside the mainstream parties, headed as they invariably are by Tweedle Dee and Tweedle Dum.

Major political parties of all persuasions may very well end up deeply regretting the way they have for many years abrogated their responsibility to protect the welfare of the children and families within their jurisdiction.

In contrast to the major parties, the majority of independent candidates in the two most recent Australian federal elections have at least acknowledged the failure of current family and child-protection policies and expressed an interest in drawing attention to worsening family justice outcomes as a matter of major concern.

The resulting outcome would certainly suggest family and child-protection issues are likely to feature far more prominently in the years ahead.

For the sake of children caught in the middle of adult power plays, it is hoped that once all the facts on family violence are presented in a balanced and honest manner and includes challenging the unac-

---

63 Arndt, op. cit., 2015.

ceptably prejudiced behaviour of authorities, the voting public will no longer tolerate the hysterical witch-hunts that currently drive the debate and inflict so much damage.

At this point, however, in the year 2018, the domestic violence sector is able to present misinformation and half-truths as fact and distort reality at will.

The electorate are told lies by both commission and omission, while taxpayers are defrauded to the tune of $22 billion each year to help fund thousands of minor children being placed into the care of unsafe legal guardians, leaving them isolated from protective family members to survive the best way they can.

Ten

The Radicalisation of Our Children

IN ITS FUNDAMENTAL form, radicalisation can best be described as the end process of a psychological power struggle for the minds of the vulnerable. One indoctrinated individual or group comes to adopt increasingly extreme political, social, or religious ideals and aspirations, imposed on them overtly or covertly by another individual or group. It is designed to destroy individual identity, purpose, independence and freedom of choice.

Today, an anxious world is desperately searching for ways to prevent the radicalisation of its young men and women, the impact of which, in one of its most extreme forms, is the ability to turn them into robotic human bombs. Within weeks, once perfectly sensible, happy young people become willing to make the ultimate sacrifice for a cause they do not understand. [64]

How does this happen? It is not just counter-insurgency experts struggling with the difficulties of deprogramming the indoctrinated.

---

64 Argus, Chris, "Radicalisation and Violent Extremism: Causes and Responses", NSW Parliamentary Research Service, Feb. 2016. Accessed here: https://www.parliament.nsw.gov.au/researchpapers/Documents/radicalisation-and-violent-extremism-causes-and-/Radicalisation%20eBrief.pdf

An unsuspecting community also concerned about the re-socialisation of its children, might do well to look closer to home for answers. It is simply wrong to assume that radicalisation is a new phenomenon brought to bear in these heightened times of religious and ideological conflict.

Isolation from any rational influence of protective family members and intense repetitive messaging, are the two most fundamental requirements for the successful rewiring of the brain. Numerous studies have shown that to re-socialise and subsequently radicalise those thus targeted is remarkably easy.

The objective is to create a false perception of reality within a distorted world view manufactured and imposed on the target, by a dominant authority, either a group or an individual.

For centuries, the military have re-socialised their recruits in boot camps, where beliefs and social values are re-engineered using intense psychological manipulation. Within six weeks new recruits, who until then had been brought up to respect the lives and rights of others, will kill a nominated enemy on command without questioning their superiors, and are prepared to lay down their own lives to do so if necessary. Such is the speed and power of persuasion.

The use of Japanese Kamikaze suicide pilots during the Second World War was a classic example of the power of indoctrination and re-socialisation. It was followed by their radicalisation and subsequent martyrdom as expendable indoctrinated military recruits, sacrificed for the benefit of a misguided cause.

When talented re-socialised student pilots were asked to volunteer for the special suicide attack force, all of the pilots would raise both of their hands, eagerly volunteering to join suicide missions. Once the rewiring of their brains was complete, radicalised recruits complied with any order, without question.

Combatants facing each other in contemporary theatres of war sing from the same sacrificial song book as their military predecessors, with each side prepared to martyr their re-socialised recruits for their particular cause.

The military are not alone, however, in messing around with the minds of their devotees or those in their care. A wide range of cults, egocentric parents, criminal gangs, religious orders, political parties, radical ideologues, relational partners, as well as media advertising and marketing gurus, are also actively engaged in the attempted rewiring of our thought processes. Their primary objective is to first entice a target into their own sphere of influence and once entrapped, to make it extremely difficult for the target to leave or express an autonomous opinion.

Religious indoctrination has the added advantage of a particularly powerful and persuasive promise of eternal life, an "afterlife" pull-factor that religious programmers use to entrap and indoctrinate the vulnerable young.

"Once we train their minds, they'll never change until they die," says the dean of the Red Mosque madrasa casually and, for the viewer, chillingly, in *Among the Believers*, a documentary on Islamist radicalisation in Pakistan.[65] It clearly illustrates how isolation from family and intense repetitive messaging works to re-socialise their targets

---

65 Jaworowski, Ken, "Review: In 'Among the Believers,' a Cleric Holds Sway," *The New York Times*. 29 Sep. 2016. Accessed here: https://www.nytimes.com/2016/09/30/movies/among-the-believers-review.html

and turn them into robotic chattels of a controlling authority. What this documentary also demonstrates is how, once indoctrinated into a cultic religious sect, parents will readily hand over their children to be re-socialised by the same authority that controls every aspect of their own lives.

But the rewiring of the brain does not occur without its problems and has disturbing consequences. Many of the psychologically entrapped such as, but not limited to military recruits, eventually go on to suffer post-traumatic stress disorder, now commonly known by its abbreviation, PTSD. Unfortunately, most of those who are psychologically stressed are not deprogrammed, prior to their exit or discharge from the source of their affliction. To a certain degree this is perfectly understandable, since it would be extremely difficult for the military for instance, to admit their actions and say, "sorry but we screwed around with your brain to ensure that our orders would never be questioned, and perhaps we should have deprogrammed you before we propelled you back into civilian life". Instead, they are discharged back into a world where killing another person is a crime, while still locked in an intensely radicalised "kill-on-command" mode. The subsequent psychological struggles are well documented.

It could well be argued that military recruits voluntarily cross the threshold into a mind-control environment, while in other settings, the civilian population is targeted involuntarily. But how many of those recruits would be aware of their impending re-socialisation and radicalisation when they sign up?

On the other hand, how many people would be aware of their imminent subjugation caused by the use of covert indoctrination techniques, when they agree to join extremist religious cults, fundamentalist political parties, and radical ideological groups? Or perhaps worse, are left in the care of malicious legal guardians, or enter into intimate relationships with attractive or charming, but deceptively manipulative, bullies?

Not for the first time, we were perplexed. With so much publicly available information on mind-control techniques and the many environments in which they are applied, why are our governments not being honest with us? Surely this is not what democracy should be about? Could all the secrecy we encountered be designed to stifle public dissent perhaps?

And most importantly, why have we, the people in the so-called civilised, developed countries of the world, not been told of our exposure to the Machiavellian practices of so many of our once respected government and private institutions, particularly, since it is we who bear the consequences?

By this time, however, we were no longer surprised to once again find official explanations blocked by an impenetrable, government-created wall of silence in the shape of secrecy requirements, suppression orders and freedom of information laws.

Such legal blockades not only prevent us from learning the truth, they also ensure the public is left well and truly in the dark about the extent of government complicity in the covert manipulation of so many of their constituents. But, those so targeted also happen to be our family, friends, neighbours and workmates. These are the people who we respect and care about the most. Is it not incumbent on those who have become aware of what is happening, therefore, to draw attention to the dangers hidden within our government's social policy frameworks and warn those we claim to care about?

While most recent media attention has been focussed on the barbaric and grotesque behaviour of radicalised Islamist youths in far off foreign lands, those engaging in a host of government-supported manipulative practices, leading to the radicalisation of so many of the young within our own communities, are allowed to peddle their destructive messages virtually unchallenged.

But how does all this relate to the subject of this book? Why is the re-socialising and subsequent radicalisation of children, considered so important within the context of child-removal policies? What has it got to do with family and child-protection policies? The answer is simple and can be described in one word, "everything". The insidious rewiring of vulnerable children's brains is one of the key drivers that initiate and enhance the family alienation process and serves to assist those engaged in the murky area of removing children from the protection of their biological families.

There are many deceitful means by which society's children are being manipulated in order to help sustain the authority and economic wealth of a contemptible child-removal industry. Forgotten by most are the personal accounts of the stolen generations of Australian Aboriginal and Torres Strait Islander descent and of the children taken from their single mothers at birth, or those of the alleged "orphans" transported from Britain to its distant colonies. At the time, all of these children were likewise told by devious government appointed legal guardians, that their parents and families were either dead, inferior, or had abandoned them. Removed and isolated from their biological families, they were prevented from learning the truth and had no way of knowing they were in fact stolen from their birth families by agents collecting children for government institutions.

Never forgotten will be the more recent conga lines of hypocritical heads of government and an assorted collection of political opportunists, representing Australia, Canada, Britain and the US, who not long ago lined up to shed crocodile tears and apologise for the child-removal policies of their predecessors, while at the same time steadfastly ignoring the identical child-removal policies and practices being imposed by their own governments.[66]

Comprehensive impact assessments on the devastating consequences of their policies either do not exist or are kept from the public by those in fear of a public backlash. What is well known, however, is the fact that any attempt to bring these unscrupulous mind-control practices to the attention of those able to question them publicly, have so far fallen on deaf ears. Shamefully, there is no political or media interest to even consider the *possibility* of bringing this issue to the forefront of child-protection policy discussions. Yet, these deplorable actions are perpetrated against the nations' children and families in breach of our fundamental human and civil rights.

But the clock is ticking, and sooner or later the house of cards will fall.

Bordering on the criminal is the fact that a mountain of available evidence in support of the claims made by millions of families and children around the world about the manipulative radicalising practices

---

66 "Children of the State", Audio Podcast, MP3, Part 1, Part 2, Part 3, Part 4. www.familybriefing.com.

employed by malicious parents and zealous bureaucrats, continues to be ignored.

The practice of using personal grievance in the radicalisation process should not be underestimated. Particularly, since it figures prominently within the dynamics of contemporary family and child-protection legislation and its devastating outcomes.

Legislation that effectively provides one parent with total control over every aspect of the lives of the family's children, and in so doing, allows that parent to eliminate the other parent out of the children's lives, is a very real phenomenon that has created a dangerous cohort of vindictive single-parent households. Children left to fend for themselves in their care, have no one else to turn to and many feel alone, isolated and abandoned. They are often exposed to real dangers, which they are forced to face the best way they can after losing the protection and support of their absent parents and other important biological family members.

The emphasis is generally on revenge for real or perceived harm inflicted by the removed parent. Once an allegation is made, however, it often goes on to trigger other psychodynamic mechanisms, such as thinking and acting within a starker "them against us" mentality. It also begins to lower the victims' inhibitions to violence and lessens incentives to avoid violence. When a child only has access to one parent's social environment, that parent gains a total control that a powerless child is unable to escape.

Over the many years of gathering information, we have found that possibly the most damaging of the countless debilitating psychological abuses perpetrated against both, the stolen children and their arbitrarily removed parents, grandparents and extended family members, is the re-socialisation and radicalisation process. Within the context of family and child-protection terminology, this process is commonly referred to as Parental Alienation.

While an unfamiliar term within the broader community, Parental Alienation is a well-documented, extremely destructive and dangerous version, of the re-socialisation and subsequent radicalisation process which follows it, and occurs to varying degrees in the vast majority of single-parent families.

Most often it is the first and most painful and disabling of the incapacitating experiences that follow. The resulting level of emotional pain experienced by the children and their absent family members is so intense as to drive many beyond the limits of their physical and psychological endurance.

Parental Alienation refers to the process and result of intense psychological manipulation of a child, which causes it to show unwarranted, as opposed to justifiable, fear, disrespect or hostility towards a biological parent or other family members. It is a distinctive and widespread form of psychological abuse and constitutes family violence towards both the child and the rejected biological family members.

Such induced psychological and emotional trauma can cause numerous health problems for those targeted, which go on to burden already stressed national health budgets.

Commonly, the primary cause is a vindictive parent wishing to exclude another parent from the life of their child. However, other family members or friends, as well as professionals involved with the family, may also be instigators. These may include psychologists, lawyers, judges and participating child-removal agencies, all of whom stand to gain from the process.

As a particularly adverse childhood experience, it often leads to the long-term or even permanent estrangement of a child from an absent parent and other family members and can result in a significantly increased risk of a range of psychosomatic illnesses for children stolen from their families.

Deeply worrying is the frightening speed by which children can be manipulated to act as robotic extensions of a malicious controlling parent and turn against an absent parent and other previously loved family members.

The ease and swiftness by which the rewiring of the developing brains of young children can occur, was discovered in 1968, when American primary school teacher Jane Ellis, conducted a now famous exercise with her third graders the day following the assassination of Dr Martin Luther King.

Known as the Brown Eyes/Blue Eyes exercise,[67] Jane Ellis has since demonstrated this exercise in many other settings around the world. As can be seen in the footage of the original exercise, in just 30 minutes these children were changed from beautiful well-behaved kids, into little Nazis who had lost all respect for their classmates, because of their eye colour.[68]

In 2018, the full extent of the well-documented, large-scale psycho-

---

67 Brown eyes and blue eyes Racism experiment (Children Session) – Jane Elliot, YouTube https://www.youtube.com/watch?v=KHxFuO2Nk-0, published by Faheem Shuaibe 24 July 2016.

68 US Public Broadcasting Service, "A Class Divided", *Frontline*, Season 3, Episode 9, accessed from YouTube, "SES 360 A CLASS DIVIDED", published by Mark Stefanovich, 5 September 2017.

logical manipulation of minor children and their radicalisation and subsequent removal from family protection, remains largely misunderstood in the broader community. Up to now, it has been an issue extremely difficult to articulate to an unwary, apathetic populace.

The message about the widespread use of such damaging psychological experimentation, not only within government bureaucracies and institutions, but also behind closed doors within many dysfunctional households, fails to be elevated to the top of the social justice policy agenda. Yet, these abhorrent practices need to be openly discussed and become part of the public discourse if we are even remotely serious about bringing to a halt their extensive use in the current large-scale removal of children from the protection of their family.

Within many areas of our daily lives, we are constantly bombarded by covert media marketing campaigns designed to either gain our support for a particular worldview or separate us from our loved ones, property or savings. The dangers lurking in the power of persuasion are grossly underestimated, except by those engaged in the psychological mind-game business. Likewise, there is very little understanding by the average person about the processes and techniques of re-socialising and radicalisation, also known as brainwashing, indoctrination, programming, coaching, coercive persuasion or manipulative thought reform. Nor is there much community awareness about the perilous phenomenon of trauma bonding and parental alienation practices.

Providing the perfect platform from which to launch the re-socialising and subsequent radicalisation process are the complex, interrelated child and family-protection systems. Laws created more than 40 years ago have legitimised an unprecedented level of kinship destruction.

These laws undermine the core principles of the Universal Declaration of Human Rights and the United Nations Convention on the Rights of the Child.

Yet, when confronted by an abundance of reliable, but currently unfashionable, academic research showing the frightening ease and speed by which radicalised thinking can be implanted into the developing brains of young children, the well-oiled propaganda machine of the child-removal sector, is quick to dismiss any factual evidence pointing to the existence of harmful child-radicalisation practices, as "junk science". But these dismissals are, in turn, the psychobabble of both the ignorant and the manipulative.

The fact that the media has failed to challenge the sector's dismissive assertions, also reflects badly on the poor state of contemporary reporting of critical newsworthy events affecting a quarter of the population.

Those who continue to remain sceptical of the powers of psychological re-socialisation practices in western democracies would do well to become acquainted with the details of the "Brown Eyes/Blue Eyes" exercises conducted by Elliot and the following well known examples of mind control and trauma bonding situations and their consequences.

Stanley Milgram, a psychologist at Yale University in the US, conducted an experiment in May 1962 on compliance with directions from authority figures. The now famous "Obedience" study showed how the power of authority can convince ordinary people to inflict terrible harm on others without hesitation. This experiment was replicated 50 years later with similar results.⁶⁹

Stanford University psychologist Philip Zimbardo directed the famous Stanford Prison Experiment in 1971 to research the influence of circumstances on the behaviour of people. (Zimbardo was also called as a specialist witness for the security guards of the Abu Graib prison in Iraq). *The experiment was stopped after only six days, because even in that short time, the guards became sadistic and the prisoners rebelled, showed signs of extreme stress, and after further repression, became depressed, believing they could not leave.*⁷⁰ ⁷¹

The Stockholm Syndrome, is a phenomenon that got its name when in 1973 a bank robber in Sweden held four hostages captive for six days during a robbery attempt. A close relationship developed with the captives, a condition that gives the syndrome its name. It is a type of emotional trauma-bonding that is in reality a survival strategy for victims of emotional and physical abuse beyond hostages to battered partners, abused or alienated children and even prisoners of war.⁷²

Patricia Hearst was the 19-year-old heiress who stunned the American nation when she turned up as a bank robber, a mere two months

---

69 "ABC (American Broadcasting Company) Channel's Milgram Experiment remake", accessed from YouTube, published by Korlan Syzdykova, 31 July 2014. For the full text of Milgram's original research, see: Milgram, Stanley, "Behavioral Study of Obedience", *Journal of Abnormal and Social Psychology*, vol. 67, no. 4, 1963, pp. 371-378., library.nhsggc.org.uk/mediaAssets/Mental Health Partnership/Peper 2 27th Nov Milgram Study KT.pdf.

70 VPRO *Backlight* (Dutch public broadcasting organisation documentary TV series), "Interview with Psychologist Phillip Zimbardo on the Stanford prison experiment", accessed from YouTube, published by VPRO Extra, 7 April 2011.

71 BBC Documentary, *The Stanford Prison Experiment* (2002), accessed from YouTube, published by "TheAnswerto1984is", 24 September 2011.

72 Van Zandt, Clint. "Why We Love the Ones Who Hurt Us: Victims of Abuse Suffer from the Stockholm Syndrome Too" *The Abrams Report*, NBC News, 13 June 2005, 11:02:33 AM ET.

after she was kidnapped by the violent cult that called itself the (United Federated Forces of the) Symbionese Liberation Army SLA). Her remarkably rapid transformation under duress was documented by bank cameras on April 15, 1974. Typical mind-control techniques, applied in a power differential environment, saw Hearst endure a cycle of isolation, threats and humiliation, which was punctuated by a little peace as a reward for compliance. This process quickly broke Hearst's sense of self and left her without any free will of her own.[73]

Parental Alienation[74] is the name given to the same cultic radicalisation phenomenon when it occurs within the context of relationship breakdown. It begins with the legitimised kidnapping of the family's children by a vindictive parent. Presently, malicious parents are able to do so using any number of government-created legal loopholes, which exist within current legislation. The alienating parent, applying the same methods used by controlling cult leaders, subsequently begins a process of manipulation and radicalisation of their children, who within a surprisingly short time will denigrate and reject their once-loved absent parent and other extended family members.[75]

Much of this research was carried out either shortly before or around the time when contemporary family and child-protection laws were enacted. In fact, dangerously unsafe legislation was created

---

[73] Morabito, Stella. "Cults in Our Midst: Patty Hearst and the Brainwashing of America." *The Federalist*, FDRLST Media, 15 April 2014, thefederalist.com/2014/04/15/cults-in-our-midst-patty-hearst-and-the-brainwashing-of-america/.

[74] Baker, Amy J.L. "The Cult of Parenthood: A Qualitative Study of Parental Alienation." *Cultic Studies Review*, vol. 4, no.1, Feb. 2005, International Cultic Studies Association, accessed at: drive.google.com/file/d/0B4dmoPK1tYNjRE8xT0xfV2hNVGs/edit.

[75] Singer, Margaret T. Dr. (writer and presenter, and Lexon Inc. (producer). *What Is A Cult and How Does It Work?* (1994), International Cultic Studies Association (ICSA), 12 Oct. 2014, www.youtube.com/watch?v=8bRBFhMEQFk.

by bureaucrats, academics, in-house lawyers and members of legal affairs committees, who at the time, would not have been aware of the dreadful psychological impact their laws were to inflict on the future generations of children and families they were designed to protect.

We are now also aware that, contrary to popular belief, a deliberately targeted covert indoctrination process can begin long before radicalisation is even attempted. The gradual radicalisation through activities that incrementally narrow a child's social circle, narrows their mindset, and in some cases, desensitises them to violence. Once the physical and psychological control over the life of a child has been surrendered to a controlling authority, however, there is very little anyone can do to alert the child victim to the potentially dangerous situation they could be entrapped in.

Not much will change however, until a tipping point is reached at which the overwhelming evidence of wrongdoing is challenged at grass-roots level and calls for accountability can no longer be ignored.

In the meantime, vulnerable children and their families will continue to be manipulated by the unscrupulous exploiters of crumbling family and child-protection systems, fractured beyond repair.

Since they can count on the apathy and general lack of interest within our communities, emboldened child removers are allowed to keep on removing the nations' children from the protection of their family with absolute impunity.

As happened throughout challenging periods of child removal in past generations, many thousands of well-meaning people are also engaged in the removal of either their own or other people's children from their families. Naively, many will be convinced that they are actually helping those children escape terrible domestic situations. Just as occurred in earlier times however, in due course many of those children will be found to have been removed on the basis of false allegations of abandonment, neglect, abuse or violence, or due to the unscrupulous behaviour of overzealous government agents taking advantage of outrageously flimsy definitions of vulnerability.

Whether they like it or not and irrespective of whether they decide to remain silent or not, those turning a blind eye today will be seen as cowardly and complicit tomorrow, while apologies will be made for their silence in the face of so much evidence of immoral conduct.

Presently on any given day, an estimated 830,000 Australian children are deprived of the protection of their biological families, while 1,000 suppression orders effectively prevent the public from learning the truth.

However, until society is able to provide every child with the legal means to escape an unsafe environment, at risk and defenceless children will continue to be used as a commodity for the unprincipled to exploit.

And their radicalisation is an essential part of that process. There are two unmistakable commonalities that most of these situations share.

First of all, in each and every different setting involving children, there exists a power differential that is being abused by a person or group to exercise total control over other people's lives.

Secondly, in each and every such setting, the abuse of that power differential is sanctioned in one form or another by government legislation.

Those abusing such power do so because they can.

Eleven

Parens Patriae – The Missing Link

AND THEN WE FOUND IT!

Finally Family Briefing discovered that the children, families and general population of most nation states have been deviously lied to by their popularly elected governments for the past 400 years, about what in effect amounts to the national legal ownership of a country's children. Successive governments have lied to their citizenry by omission for the past four centuries, in order to make it easier to remove their nation's children from their families.

A watershed moment came with the realisation that, contrary to popular belief, all children are in fact the property of the State. Central to resolving our inability to adequately protect minor children from abuse and neglect is our failure to recognise the harmful omnipotence of a little known 16th Century English doctrine – parens patriae. This doctrine has been used by nation states for the past four centuries to legitimise the removal of generations of children from the native populations of the colonial empires, remove thousands of babies from their mothers at birth and banish thousands of children from England to the colonies by labelling them "orphans".

All of those children had one thing in common: they were declared "vulnerable" and therefore in need of State "protection", thus triggering the supreme guardianship parens patriae powers of the State.

Since then, and now well into the 21st Century, the parens patriae doctrine continues to be in widespread use by nation states. It serves to deprive children of their liberty for purported protective purposes, and legitimises the unrelenting removal of those children from their families for redistribution. In so doing, it is creating one stolen generation after another, for profit.

Irrespective of race, gender or colour but bound together in grief, children and parents continue to have no legal right to the protection of their biological family. Any protective guardianship responsibilities that families may think they have can be revoked at any time with ease. Children can be removed from their families using the flimsiest allegations of abuse, and so activate the parens patriae doctrine which then goes on to produce the next stolen generation of "vulnerable" children.

In 2018, the State continues to apply these powers to decide who such "vulnerable" children will live with and who is to protect them from harm. Powerless biological parents and families are forced to stand by helplessly and are expected to accept without question the loss of their children and the fact they are no longer able to protect them from harm. For many millions of fit parents and families around the world, the future well-being of their children is now out of their hands and decided by an integrated network of government institutions, delegated government employees and co-opted charities, and NGOs. These organisations and individuals are all free to control other people's children on the oft-abused prescription, "the best interests of the child."

This is how history keeps repeating itself; governments are in fact able to operate as a dictatorship within a democracy.

The State's parens patriae powers have provided governments with the legal authority to remove "its" children from their families, as they see fit.

Successive governments have for many years expanded the use of these powers into a range of other areas, extending control over their constituents. The shift, from using not-for-profits to for-profit corporations to manage the lives of children removed from their families, has effectively turned child-protection practices into modern day slave markets.

One of the most remarkable things about this long-running debate is not just the way sophisticated and unbiased discussion has been trammelled, but powerful bureaucracies' and institutions' resistance to any change. Enquiry after enquiry, book after book, critic after critic have exposed some horrendous legitimised abuses by contemporary democracies and their child-protection systems, without result.

Poor, or in many cases demonstrably counterproductive, results have never been seen as good enough reason to actually fix the problem, abolish or reform the institutions involved, or reach sensible legislative solutions unhindered by ideology. Many of the social and economic costs have been recognised for decades, but nothing has changed. Governments have never been held to account, with secrecy provisions and suppression orders making sure of such shielding from responsibility.

It is as if we have created a war zone where kids have become collateral damage. But, somewhere along the line, we always thought, something *has* to change, that something *would* change, and in the end, something *did* change.

That moment came when, as outlined, we stumbled across the parens patriae doctrine and how the State has been able to gift itself so much power over the lives of parents and children for the past 400 years.

While we have finally been able to put the big-picture jigsaw puzzle together, the final piece of that puzzle had proved extremely elusive. Now more than 12 years after we began our search, I must admit there were a number of times when we actually thought we had found the catalyst for the chaos created by contemporary family and child-protection systems. Only to discover that what we had considered to be the principal causal factor, was simply another of the many consequential effects. We knew very well that after all is said and done, if we had not been able to link everything we had discovered back to a single origin, every one of our findings would have been inconsequential. Simply put, it is impossible to cure cancer by only removing secondary tumours, or expecting to cure a skin cancer by repetitively covering it with fresh surgical dressings.

It was certainly good to have been able to create a benchmark that would enable future policymakers to more accurately measure the success or failure of their policies. It was also an encouraging achievement that we were able to provide better estimates of taxpayer-funded socioeconomic costs, as well as point out the full extent of the social consequences that current policies and practices are inflicting on the electorate. But without that elusive link, appropriate legislative solutions would have remained very difficult to create.

Eventually, we reached a point where we realised that the fundamental question posed by Tony Coe back in London in the summer of 2007, as to what *legal parenting rights parents actually have to parent their own biological children,* had still not been answered. Since it had become the trigger for an exhaustive search for such a missing link, we were disappointed that we had still not been able to find it. It was certainly not for the lack of trying, but up to that point, our search had remained stubbornly unsuccessful. We had tried everything to get someone to provide a definitive answer as to what legal parenting rights parents have. The response had always been the same, either no answer at all, or an evasive, carefully structured reference to parental responsibility. When we changed the question slightly by asking if parents had any legal parenting rights at all, and that a simple *yes* or *no* would suffice, there was still never any answer. We had also joined legal discussion forums and approached the subject many times, only to receive the same resolute silent treatment from the legal profession. Interestingly nevertheless, this did do one thing; it increased our suspicion that the legal profession may have been hiding something which they preferred the public not to know.

It is not too difficult to see why, since most people considering the option of seeking a just outcome using the current family justice system already see it as an exercise in futility.

But why all the fuss some would say? Why was it so important to find out what, if any, legal parenting rights millions of mothers and fathers might have?

The answer to that is relatively simple. Without the capacity to lay claim to any legal rights, anyone seeking justice in a court of law will fail. Any court of law that considers you have no legal rights can be judged a Kangaroo Court by its own definition, since it is a court of law in which the flagrant violations of procedure, precedent, due process and essential human rights are so gross, that fundamental justice and the rule of law are denied.

Families who have experienced their children being removed by government commissioned agents throughout the past 400 years, have not been able to apply to any court of justice for their return since they are considered to have no legal ownership or parenting rights over their own children. We now know, that this situation continues to exist today because in law, every child remains the property of their nation's government. The State claims this through parens patriae.

The question of legal parenting rights therefore remains absolutely crucial to the whole debate today. We have always considered the answer to that question as irrefutably representing the "biggest fish of a thousand casts".

We stumbled across the answer we were looking for completely by chance. It was during one of those moments in time when all the planets lined up to reveal what for so long had escaped our attention.

Out of frustration, it had been decided to go back and dig into the mountain of information collected over the years to see if we could find something we might have missed.

References to parens patriae had been briefly looked at some years back, but at the time, and in isolation, they had not seemed relevant to the answers we were so desperately seeking. Perhaps instinctively, they had been put aside, considered worthy of revisiting down the track. Also, we had been aware for a long time that there is a legal duty of care for parents and extended family members to responsibly parent the family's biological children, and that at all times such parenting is to consider the children's "best interests" as paramount.

But one night in July of 2017, as I was watching an ABC TV *Lateline* program while at the same time trying to read through some information on the parens patriae doctrine, program host Emma Alberici asked her guest, Professor Penney Lewis, co-director of the Centre of Medical Law and Ethics at Kings College London, the following question: *"What does the law tell us about who is deemed to be the ultimate judge of what's in the best interests of a child."*[76]

The professor chose her words carefully: *"Parents have the responsibilities to make decisions on behalf of their children and the presumption is that parents make those decisions in their child's best interests. It's only in very, very rare cases where there's some question about whether the parents are making a decision that's in their child's best interests, that courts become involved.*

It was then, that I realised just how intrinsically enmeshed "parental responsibility" and parens patriae are. I also became aware that the significance should not be underestimated, since the supreme guardianship powers of the state inherent in the parens patriae principle provide national governments with a power differential over its citizens like no other.

---

76 Alberici, Emma. *Interview: Professor Penney Lewis, Medical Ethicist.* ABC Lateline, Australian Broadcasting Corporation Television, 26 July 2017, 10.01pm. Full Transcript: www.abc.net.au/lateline/interview:-professor-penney-lewis,-medical-ethicist/8746982.

It is in fact the mother of all power differential controls, when used to remove children from their parents. And, instead of only happening "very, very, rarely" as the professor asserted, it happens in *each and every contested case*.

In Australia alone, with a current child population of 5.2 million, this power differential equates to a ratio of 5.2 million to nil excluding their equally powerless parents and extended family members.

While our political leadership is quick to claim we are a nation of laws, this established legal power differential can hardly be considered credible for a country that prides itself on a strong belief in the rule of law and is constantly repeating pro-family mantras. Neither does it present a level playing field for families seeking justice in our courts.

The underlying reason for their powerlessness may have puzzled dispossessed families for centuries, but not those who have exploited such lack of parental rights for either profit or parental dominance.

Also at that moment, it became patently obvious that we might have been asking the wrong question all along. The question that conceivably should have been asked is: *"What gives governments the legal right to remove children from their biological parents?"* Perhaps the answer may have been much more forthcoming, since it has been staring everyone in the face the whole time.

But then again, if the broader electorate were to discover contemporary governments have been removing and redistributing their children since 1975 due to families being officially rendered powerless to prevent it, faith in our governments would be lost and very likely many politicians' re-election prospects would begin to look pretty grim.

For the past 400 years, nation states have knowingly seen fit to remove millions of children from their families, while watching their countries' despairing families plead with government institutions and agencies to retain their children or be reunited with those earlier stolen from their care and protection. They have done so in the full knowledge that it is only the state that can claim the right to legal ownership and guardianship of a nation's children, provided they are categorised as "vulnerable" first. The continuously changing definition, of this "vulnerability" status, has ensured a guaranteed supply of children for the enabling institutions representing the child-removal sector.

In addition, the involvement of a large number of jurisdictions and infrastructures and a plethora of laws relating to children's welfare, have all combined to provide a constantly changing legislative climate. These factors in turn impact upon practices and outcomes.

In 2010, the Australian Law Reform Commission (ALRC) produced a report for the then Australian attorney-general, in which the supreme guardianship powers of the state and their intersection with family and child-protection laws were clearly acknowledged.

> The state, as parens patriae, and the family intersect in the arena of child protection. Child protection 'intervention' may place a parent in opposition to the state, expressed in terms of a parent 'losing' his or her children. As the state, through child protection agencies, is a principle 'actor', child protection law can be characterised as 'public' law, in contrast to the 'private' law of family law, considered above.[77]

---

[77] Australian Law Reform Commission and New South Wales Law Reform Commission. *Family violence: A National Legal Response: Final Report*. Section 4.60, p. 171. Sydney, 2010.

Many other references can be found, particularly in government publications, which also refer to the legal authority conferred on national governments by the doctrine of parens patriae and how its powers are used in the family and child-protection jurisdictions.[78] In contrast, what remains particularly obvious is the fact that any reference to any possible legal rights of parents to protect and parent their own biological children is non-existent and emphasises the futility of seeking such rights in our courts.

The parens patriae powers of the state arrived in Australia with the First Fleet and have created havoc among every population group ever since:

> Parents are required to act in the child's best interests and, if there is any doubt about whether a parent's decision accords with this, then any person who is concerned about the child's welfare or treatment may apply to a court to intervene. The state acts as the protector of children in the interests of society. This is called the parens patriae jurisdiction of the court and springs from the direct responsibility of the Crown to look after those who are unable to care for themselves.[79]

But what exactly is this all-pervading, monolithic 16th Century parens patriae doctrine that is still providing governments in the 21st

---

78 Finch, Katherine Patricia. "Decisions on Behalf of Your Children: The Doctrine of 'Parens Patriae' in Australia." *Family Law Express*, 4 Mar. 2014, 00:12:44, www.familylawexpress.com.au/family-law-brief/children/parentalresponsibility/parens-patriae/decisions-on-behalf-of-your-children-the-doctrine-of-parens-patriae-in-australia/2238/.

79 "Citizen Child: Australian Law and Children's Rights." Edited by Kathleen Funder, Australian Institute of Family Studies, Australian Government, Dec. 1996, /publications/citizen-child-australian-law-and-childrens-rights. Archived publication

Century the authority to remove millions of children from the protection of their families?

Invoked by the King's Bench[80] in the 16th Century, parens patriae is Latin for "parent of the nation" and in law refers to the common law doctrine by which the Sovereign has an obligation to protect the interests of those unable to protect themselves. The concept was restricted to the mentally incompetent, but by 1608, the Lord Chancellor had extended it to include vulnerable children as well. The protection of the mentally ill and abused or neglected children was gradually applied throughout the 17th and 18th centuries and beyond.

It has since evolved from granting absolute rights to the sovereign, to one that is more associated with the rights and obligation of nation states and their courts, towards vulnerable children and incapacitated adults.

Parens patriae is a doctrine that has vested in the state the supreme guardianship authority to protect individuals who are deemed legally unable to act on their own behalf. When a government exercises its parens patriae powers, it assumes the role of guardian acting on behalf of either a child or mentally disabled individual. The use of foster homes and other shelters is an example of how family courts use the parens patriae doctrine.

When a child is removed from his or her home in accordance with the parens patriae doctrine, the government must act in accordance with "the best interests of the child". This allows governments to

---

80 The King's Bench was one of the highest British courts of appeal dealing with mainly criminal matters until it was merged by the Supreme Court of Judicature Act 1873 into a single High Court of Justice. The King's Bench ceased to exist, except as the King's Bench (now Queen's Bench) Division of the High Court.

assume both legal and physical custody of any child in question evaluated as "vulnerable". Any subsequent person or persons appointed by any government to assume the role of legal guardian on its behalf, is also allowed to make significant decisions on behalf of that child or adult. Nevertheless, when governments, or any number of their agents or institutions, delegate the task of managing the upbringing of children to others, such as either one of the biological parents or foster parents, the government retains full legal custody and accepts complete responsibility over those children.

Ultimately, the state has the highest authority to act as guardian of all children residing within its jurisdictions. State courts have the inherent authority to intervene to protect the best interests of children when their well-being is seen as at risk by harmful acts, such as neglect or abuse. The full extent of this authority is defined within legislation around child protection.

That the parens patriae powers of the state were going to be the catalyst for abuse of the vulnerable and inflict untold damage upon powerless families for centuries to come, in hindsight, was evident almost from the start.

Within just a few short years of vulnerable children being added to the parens patriae powers of the state, unscrupulous child removers began to take advantage and ply their ghastly trade, when Britain began exporting shiploads of allegedly "orphaned children" to far-flung British colonies. The practice began in 1618 when a group of "orphaned and destitute" children left Britain for Richmond, Virginia in the US.

This was the start of a regrettable period in British history, which is now referred to as Britain's child-migration scheme.[81] For three and a half centuries, boatloads of "vulnerable" British children were transported to Canada, New Zealand, South Africa, Australia, Rhodesia (now Zimbabwe) and the Caribbean. These poor children were sent overseas with no further arrangements to inspect their progress, check on their welfare or give them access to personal and family records. It has left a legacy of cruelty, lies and deceit. Children were told their parents were dead, that they came from deprived backgrounds or that they were rescued and should be grateful. Yet most of these children were not orphans and the families they came from were neither poor nor deprived.

Margaret Humphreys is a highly decorated British social worker whose investigations led to the exposure of the child-migration scheme in two major articles in *The Observer* newspaper in July 1987. We contacted the journalist Annabel Ferriman, who wrote the articles that exposed *that* particular period of child removals to the world, as part of the research for this book. She was kind enough to supply copies of the original articles to assist us with additional historic background information for this book. Humphreys also wrote *Empty Cradles*, which was first published in 1994, about her investigations into what happened to the children shipped to Australia.[82] A film about her investigations titled *Oranges and Sunshine* followed in 2010.

The last of the child-migrant ships sailed for Australia in 1967. It took almost 350 years to stop the practice and somehow the world is of the impression that since then, all such child removals have stopped.

---

81 Bean, Phillip, and Joy Melville. *Lost Children of the Empire: The Untold Story of Britain's Child Migrants*. Unwin Hyman, 1989.

82 Humphreys, Margaret. *Empty Cradles*. 1st ed., Doubleday, 1994.

Unfortunately, the abuse of government parens patriae powers by the unprincipled and immoral has never stopped – far from it. The same cruelty, lies and deceit are suffered today, only in a new setting, under a different banner, at another time. Since Australia has always retained its all-powerful parens patriae authority, the government of the day, in 1975, introduced new child-removal legislation, this time disguised as the Family Law Act. It was promoted as offering caring government help to vulnerable constituents, purportedly to assist them navigate the difficulties of relationship breakdown.

And so began the next era of child-removal policies, which by 2018 have caused more than 6 million Australians to lose the protection of their families, with an estimated 65,000 of them taking their own lives, courtesy of policy failures all made possible by the parens patriae powers of the state.

Numerous authors and critics have written about the ever expanding power of Western governments and the expansion of state power into every corner of modern life. Nowhere is this more vividly illustrated than in the contemporary debates surrounding the rapid expansion of government surveillance with terror and national security being used as excuses for the destruction of the individual's right to privacy. But equally, the power of the state to invade traditional family life has been one of the foundation planks on which vast bureaucratic, social welfare, family-court, child-support and child-protection edifices have been built. The results have been disastrous for all concerned. Women have been trapped in traditional parenting roles and fathers left heartbroken and frequently damaged for life, while the children at the crux of the matter are seriously disadvantaged by the operations of the state.

All too often, government institutions that claim to be protecting children or acting in the best interests of children are doing nothing of the kind.

What does not appear to be understood by the electorate is that every time a parent or family member alleges a case of domestic violence or abuse, they unwittingly place the families' children in danger by doing so. Domestic family violence laws consider a child in danger and therefore a victim of abuse if an allegation is made by either one of their parents against the other. They are considered in danger either from an alleged perpetrator or from a possibly perjuring accuser. Any such child is automatically considered "vulnerable" and becomes a potential victim of the parens patriae doctrine.

If anyone should have any doubt about the frightening power of the state to remove children from their families following an alleged domestic violence incident, irrespective of whether they are a victim or perpetrator, note the Donna Carson story. In that case the appalling behaviour of the Department of Community Services in its use of its parens patriae powers, resulted in the children being removed from their mother by the department after their mother was bashed and doused with petrol by her then boyfriend and set alight.

The children were removed while their mother was fighting for her life and would have been lost in the system if it were not for the tenacity of their mother. Carson not only fought a courageous battle to survive her injuries, she also challenged the right of authorities to remove her children while she was an incapacitated victim of violent physical abuse.

As it turned out, her children had far more to fear from the authority that was supposed to protect them from harm, than any perceived harm coming to them from domestic violence. Against all odds and obstacles put in her path by the child-protection authorities, who stonewalled her demands to have her children returned to her care, she eventually overcame their cruelty.

In her search for answers, Carson uncovered a web of lies, conflicting evidence, missing records, negligent investigations and "a whole lot of people who were suddenly struck deaf and dumb". She survived and went on to sue the department, had her children returned and received enough compensation to purchase a house. Donna was recognised for her courage and received an Australian of the Year, Local Hero award in 2004, and went on to write a book about her ordeal, *Judas Kisses*.[83]

Most stolen children and their missing families, simply lose the strength to mount such a challenge and suffer the loss of their loved ones in silence.

They struggle daily, with an unbearable pain life had not prepared them for.

> "To take children from their families was an Abuse"
> "To strip them of their identity was an Abuse"
> "To forget them and then deny their loss was an Abuse"
> "Within this context and within our culture, few tragedies can compare"
> Margaret Humphreys [84]

---

83 Carson, Donna. *Judas Kisses: A True Story of Betrayal and Survival.* Edited by Debbie Ritchie, 1st ed., Hardie Grant, 2007.
84 Humphreys, op. cit., 1994

Twelve

Child Protection Reform Proposal

A Time for Change

AT THE CORE OF any strong and resilient society is the safety of its children, since nothing strikes deeper into the human heart than the loss of a biological child. Profoundly embedded in our human DNA is a natural instinct that exists within every parent to protect their biological children from harm at any cost.

It is not unreasonable therefore to assume that, first and foremost, by this time every minor child should have acquired the presumption at birth of an inherent legal right to be protected by those closest to them biologically – such as each of their willing, able and fit biological parents and extended families.

But nothing could be further from the truth!

The protection of a family's children comes in two parts: those that *need* protection and those that can *provide* protection. However, for the past 400 years, we have allowed nation states to use the little known parens patriae doctrine to separate protective biological family members from their children, simply by claiming it to be "in their best interest". For those four centuries, we have failed to recognise that the resulting "vulnerable" children have consistently formed the core of one "stolen generation" after another.

Like a medieval cloud hanging over our heads, this harmful 16th Century doctrine remains in use today by 21st Century nation states in order to ensure national governments maintain their supreme guardianship powers over every child within their jurisdiction. Over time and armed with such commanding authority, successive governments have continued to produce many dubious, often ingenious new laws and practices, each one of which is designed to help create public hysteria and label increasing numbers of minor children as being vulnerable. In so doing, every one of those children are ensured of their eligibility for membership of the next stolen generation.

Although many of these laws and practices have subsequently been discredited and apologised for, while in use, each one of them served to act as a trigger to invoke the supreme parens patriae guardianship powers of the state and so generate a continues flow of new victims for decades on end. Our 400-year-long failure to recognise the severe damage we are inflicting on the most vulnerable of our fellow citizens demeans all of us.

No doubt, many of those taking part today may be well intentioned, but by their enabling association alone, everyone engaged in these practices, whether wilfully blind or blissfully ignorant, will be seen as complicit in supporting the human suffering inflicted upon each one of those stolen generations. History therefore is highly unlikely to be kind to those who remain silent in the face of the evidence before them.

Our extensive investigations have revealed a new window into the world of the contemporary family, which may help to understand what lies behind many of the headlines. The existence of a perceived lack of fairness within our communities strongly suggests an urgent need exists to change policy and make the rationale behind it more transparent, equitable and workable, for the common good. If we are really serious and consider it important to maintain a healthy, equitable society, however, then the need to engage the public has never been greater. To shine a light on the exploitation of the weak by the strong, and where necessary, on the failures of those with power to vindicate the trust placed in them, the Family Briefing team has endeavoured to bridge the gap between community misconceptions and the truth.

The main focus of this book is to document our conclusions for posterity and introduce a number of important new factors, which will need to be taken into account and considered as part of any genuine attempts to promote reform.

Since we have not shied away from being highly critical of unsavoury child-removal practices, we also considered it our duty towards all those who do not have a voice, to submit a workable child-protection-reform proposal, one that is founded on our many years of evidence-based research into the plight of defenceless children and their disempowered families. Accordingly, we would like to present the outcome of our collective considerations, and hope that it will be taken into account and play a small part in the difficult search ahead for genuine, workable, new child-protection legislation. We are all responsible for what happens next, and need to realise that we are rearing the next generation and that should we continue to fail, history will hold us accountable.

A Blueprint for Child-Protection Reform

That every 21st Century nation state, be required to provide every minor child within its jurisdiction with an inherent, legal Best Interest Birthright, that guarantees every minor child the physical and emotional protection of both of their fit biological parents and families equally.

That the following legal, protective family rights, be decreed as fundamental founding principles in law, in order to accommodate such requirement:

- That the parental status of each willing, able and fit biological parent, is legally recognised as being of equal value, and that such parental status be referred to as an "equal primary care parent".
- That every child is awarded an inherent, rebuttable, presumptive legal birthright to spend a crucial minimum percentage of physical "Protective Contact" time plus once a week phone contact, with each of their equal primary care parents or a nominated member of their biological family, unless any such contact is legitimately found to be unsafe or impractical. *(Protective Contact = 20% or more overnight stays per year)
- That the obstruction of any legitimate, protective contact or physical parenting time, by either parent, invokes a possible criminal charge of contempt of court, and/or child abduction, and/or child abuse, in order to provide an effective, practical enforcement measure.
- That all violence and/or abuse allegations are processed in the criminal justice jurisdiction, providing due process of law, a mandatory mental health screening test, and appropriate penalties for perjury.
- That any allegations of violence and/or abuse are to be accompanied by immediate court ordered secure protection, of a child's relationship with each of their equal primary care parents, until such allegations have been expertly investigated by appropriate authorities (Note the Hague Convention).
- That in the event the equal primary care parents are not able to resolve their differences due to entrenched inflexible hostility, both parents are to submit to a mandatory mental health screening test.
- That improved knowledge of trauma-bonding and the radicalisation process is acquired by family justice and child-protection authorities, in order to better understand the risks and consequences of sole custody, and of allowing minor children to express their preferred living and parenting arrangements in court-ordered assessments. Especially since there is a very real risk those children are in fact helpless victims of duress, while they are trapped in the perfect indoctrination setting provided by the present family justice system.

> * The Protective Contact benchmark of 20% or more of overnight stays per year is used, in order to better define and enhance the quality and value of such contact, and measure global outcomes. While more than 20% may increase the protective value of the contact and would be achievable for the vast majority of families, it is however only possible when geographical settings are favourable. Conversely, and irrespective of whether the geographical settings are favourable or not, it is important to note that when contact visits are progressively diminished from the 20% of protective overnight stays, they are progressively diminishing a child's protective security safety shield, as well as the opportunity to effectively bond with each of their parents equally. Physical, sexual and emotional abuse occurs out of sight of prying eyes. Early detection, which Protective Contact with biological family members provides, offers every child the best protection against any such abuse.

Following the revelation of unspeakable historical wrongs of the past, such as, but not limited to, slavery, apartheid policies, the stolen generations and the atrocities inflicted by Nazi tyranny, there were many people who said: "if only we had known, we would have spoken out". Well the world does now know what we are doing to our children and as a result, to continue to turn a blind eye is no longer a credible option.

While it took 300 years to abolish slavery, the large-scale removal of children from the protection of their biological families has been in existence for 400 years, with no end in sight.

We are not alone in pointing out the misplaced trust the community affords our political leadership and traditional media. From around the globe, anxious warnings have been sounded for many years. The outpourings of grief and despair by the victim children and families have also continued unabated.

The writings of such esteemed authors as Joseph Goldstein, Anne Freud and Albert Solnit, emphasise the importance of continuity and security in a child's upbringing:

> When family integrity is broken or weakened by State intrusion ... (The younger child's) needs are thwarted and his belief that his parents are omniscient and all powerful is shaken prematurely. The effect on the child's developmental progress is invariably detrimental. The child's needs for safety within the confines of the family must be met by law through its recognition of family privacy as the barrier to State intrusion upon parental autonomy in child rearing.[85]

UK Supreme Court justices led by Deputy President Lady Hale have associated child-removal actions of the state with the machinations of a totalitarian regime:

> The first thing that a totalitarian regime tries to do is to get at the children, to distance them from the subversive, varied influences of their families, and indoctrinate them in their rulers' view of the world. Within limits, families must be left to bring up their children in their own way.[86]

While long overdue, perhaps the time has come for a more enlightened and better informed electorate to demand of their elected representatives in national governments to at least consider the option of *curbing* the harmful parens patriae powers. Should such appeal to our national governments fail to pique their interest, the electorate itself may need to take the initiative, mobilise their people power and elect a better informed parliamentary leadership.

---

85 Goldstein, Joseph, et al. *Beyond the Best Interests of the Child.* The Free Press, New York, 1979.

86 Grant, Graham. "Named and Shamed." *Scottish Daily Mail*, p. 1, 29 July 2016, www.pressreader.com/uk/scottish-daily-mail/20160729/textview.

It can only become a reality however, when common sense triumphs and enough people come to realise that every defenceless minor child deserves to be provided with an inherent, legal "best interest" right from birth, to the guaranteed effective protection of both of their willing, able and fit biological parents and extended families equally, during their childhood. This would serve to provide a much needed practical first line of defence for every vulnerable child, and help to deter anyone who may seek to inflict physical, sexual and/or emotional abuse and neglect upon any of the nation's children.

Well respected Australian author and journalist Caroline Overington observed:

> The fact something is, doesn't mean it should be or that it shall remain so. It was once taken as a given that slaves – black human beings – had a reduced capacity for personal responsibility, compared with that of white slave owners. That was simply the way things were until we all got a hold of ourselves. Nobody would make that argument today. The way things are says nothing about the way things ought to be. It was likewise once taken as a given that it was in the best interest of Indigenous children to be removed from their families and placed into the care of white society. We now know how wrong that was, and community assumptions are that such practice ceased to exist long ago.[87]

But community assumptions that such practices ceased to exist long ago, is where community misconceptions meet reality. It is where

---

87 Overington, Caroline. "A Duty of Care to Hear More Women's Voices in Parliament." *The Weekend Australian*, 10 Sept. 2016, https://www.theaustralian.com.au/opinion/columnists/a-duty-of-care-to-hear-more-womens-voices-in-parliament/news-story/c43a28b1a2895e4ff008e0abefc22dfa

the forced removal of minor children from their biological families under the guise of a range of government-sponsored welfare criteria, is exposed and comes to a shrieking cultural reality check. The fact is the state has never stopped removing expediently categorised "vulnerable" children from their parents, irrespective of their colour, gender or ethnicity, with more children being removed from the protection of their biological family in 2018 than ever before in our history.

There are many dangers inherent in the coercive parens patriae powers of the state when used by professionals who fail to differentiate between their professional knowledge and their personal beliefs.

For powerless families, the dangers faced from professionals ruthlessly following the ideologies of their employers are immense. In the absence of adequate transparency protocols and public scrutiny, many professionals working in the contentious family and child-protection jurisdictions are able to act way beyond their authority by assuming the role of a parent. Ideally, the distinction between caring expertise and the usurpation of the parenting role, should be thoroughly understood, and at all times scrupulously maintained. But that is not what happens. As a consequence, far too often the personal ideological prejudices of the professional involved, leads to devastating outcomes for the welfare of powerless children and their families who are without rights.

Being authorised to play god with other people's children carries with it an obligation to prioritise the welfare of the child over your own, not to appease the arbiters of ideological insanity who dismiss common sense as the voice of the uneducated.

The enormous damage we are collectively inflicting on our children and our communities are detailed in this book. In the end, however, community members themselves have to find a way to eradicate the cause of their maltreatment, and it is impossible to do that unless you have a pretty good idea of what confronts you. The failure to adequately protect the nation's children belongs to all of us and it is therefore incumbent upon the whole of community to make a stand and insist we do better.

There are of course those who feel we should wait another 300 years before we act. Many of them are making a comfortable living out of other people's children and do not want to see that end. Blinded by self-interest, they are unwilling or incapable of seeing the bigger picture.

But for those interested in supporting change, a practical alternative is now available to contemplate, which may possibly provide the necessary trigger to inspire affirmative community action.

Our own reform proposal is based on all the new information that has come to light and, while it is not suggested every issue will be resolved, unless significant changes are made things will remain exactly as they are today, to the detriment of every child for generations to come.

Unless the obstacles to transparency are removed and the community is better able to scrutinise the secretive organisations, institutions, bureaucracies and agencies that target children, they cannot be held to account and will simply continue to wreak havoc on contemporary society.

A better informed electorate will need to arrive at a place where it will no longer tolerate the continuance of legitimised government cover-ups in the form of secrecy and suppression orders in order to hide government complicity.

Those who protect perpetrators of violence and/or abuse against children in other settings are increasingly being called upon to stand trial for their poor judgement and their failure to protect the children in their care. Why then do we tolerate such failings when it is our elected governments that are at the centre of such actions?

But the road to correct a gross injustice is not for the fainthearted or timid. In his letter from Birmingham jail in 1963, Dr. Martin Luther King Jr expressed deep sorrow at broader community failure to engage in the civil rights campaigns:

> I have almost reached the lamentable conclusion that the Negro's great stumbling block in the stride toward freedom is not the White Citizen's Counciler or the Ku Klux Klanner, but the white moderate, who is more devoted to "order" than to justice; who prefers a negative peace which is the absence of tension to a positive peace which is the presence of justice.[88]

Dr. Martin Luther King Jr's words are a judicious reminder that for those of us who are comfortably situated in intact relationships but no longer wish to remain silent, the task of dismantling decadent 400-year-old child-removal policies will be painful. It will involve the earning of self-respect and becoming *'comfortable with discomfort'*. It will require conflict, disorder and division from some of those we hold dear and the challenging of cherished myths.

---

[88] King, Jnr., Martin Luther. "Letter from a Birmingham Jail." Received by Bishop C.C.J. Carpenter, Bishop Joseph A. Durick, Rabbi Milton L. Grafman, Bishop Nolan B. Harmon, the Rev. George H. Murray, the Rev. Edward V. Ramage, the Rev. Earl Stallings, 16 Apr. 1963, Birmingham, Alabama. Early draft: http://okra.stanford.edu/transcription/document_images/undecided/630416-019.pdf

Thirteen

Conclusion: The Challenge

ONE THING ABOUT Groundhog Day is that you know exactly what comes next. At the time of writing, in the summer of 2018, and right on cue, vulnerable children around the globe are being removed from the protection of their biological families at precisely the same rate as they were back in the summer of 2007 when our investigative journey began.

Global societies steadfastly refuse to heed the unfashionable prophesied warnings of the destructive long-term ramifications of government child-protection failings. Even though morally unconscionable and legally indefensible, nations continue to manage relationship breakdown in a manner that ensures the destruction of kinship structures so necessary to maintain a healthy society, is fast moving past the point of no return.

History tells us that when weak and apathetic political leadership ignores all available warnings, they do so at their own peril. Once destroyed, it is virtually impossible to regain the trust and support of the civilian population to initiate the difficult programs necessary to restore a broken society into a healthy vibrant community.

Without any legal parenting rights to protect their biological offspring from harm, with very few exceptions, the vast majority of the family victims find solace in first identifying with and subsequently ending up locked into sharing their pain with a cohort of fellow victims of any one of a multitude of interconnected symptoms resulting from legitimised dispossession. Significant numbers go to their graves broken-hearted. Beaten, they remain unable or unwilling to broaden their search for the actual social disease that is the primary cause of their symptoms. Becoming keypad warriors, most are unable to shake loose from the comfort of the shared experience, firmly in the belief the answer lies in finding a way to eliminate the particular symptom that is the cause of so much of their own personal grief.

Dysfunctional courts, maladjusted child-protection agencies, extremist gender-based ideologies, all get the blame. These poor souls, mothers and fathers, many tormented by the unbearable pain of losing their children, family and possessions, struggle to function as rationally behaving and practically thinking human beings. They live to hopefully survive another day. For them, the idea of thinking proactively has been lost, often permanently. Even being reactive is generally reduced to venting their anger and feelings of despair by posting on internet forums. Since all other avenues to raise any semblance of self-esteem and self-empowerment have been taken away, this is about as close as they get to being able to maintain even a snippet of dignity and self-respect.

But the oppressed will need to find the inner strength to *demand* their freedom, since oppressors never voluntarily relinquish their power.

For the past 40 years, the debate, fuelled by some outstanding scholarly, intellectual arguments by social and legal academics, has focussed on the emotional and psychological benefits of young children preserving close biological kinship bonds with their families.[89] This has been largely ignored by governments. This book's focus, however, is very much on the important protective value of such bonds. Civil society continues to be hoodwinked into placing its trust in the misleading narrative of soulless governments.

Following the discovery of the sheer extent and magnitude by which we fail to protect minor children from harm, an urgently needed new debate, if not a Royal Commission, will sooner or later unfold. Hopefully, this will lead to urgently needed reforms.

We decided to initiate that debate and submit a reform proposal founded on non-negotiable, fundamental human rights principles of equality and justice.

It is a set of proposals that requires every nation state to ensure that every minor child within their jurisdiction will obtain an inherent, legal "best interest birthright", to the protection of all willing, able and fit members of their immediate biological family, as a first line of defence against violence, abuse and neglect during their early formative childhood years.

Any such reforms will need to be brought to the attention of the UN, human rights organisations and genuine child-protection advocates, as well as lawmakers, media and the broader civilian population.

Contemporary family and child-protection laws and practices operate in defiance of the rule of law, and we now know that as a consequence, nation states have been able to rob their population of

---

[89] Warshak, op. cit., 2017.

their entitlement to natural justice for the past 400 years using their supreme parens patriae powers.

It is not that there has been silence on these matters – far from it. It's just that almost nobody is listening. The greatest obstacle to sound policy is ignorance, and if trophies were handed out for ignorance, the perpetuation of our current family and child-protection policies and practices would win the gold medal hands down.

Government can no longer hide the fact their own data shows that since 1975, in Australia, more than 6 million family victims of the parens patriae doctrine have accumulated, with 65,000 men, women and children, estimated to have taken their own lives as a result. While at the same time it has been shown the annual cost to Australian taxpayers, is estimated to be running in excess of $53 billion per annum. All of which is craftily screened, modified or simply withheld from public scrutiny, as such information is not considered to be in the public's best interest. Founded on ignorance and protected by secrecy, many of these policies are not only breathtakingly merciless, but criminally negligent.

Their continued existence is made possible only by sustained political, media, public and religious apathy, inertia and paralysis.

Political leadership is fond of claiming its support for the rule of law and rules based systems. But these are upheld by the oath to tell the truth, the whole truth, and nothing but the truth. In reality, the civil jurisdiction of family law supports the rule of the jungle, where judicial consent upholds the oath to tell untruths, half-truths and anything but the truth. Within this troubled jurisdiction, whoever makes the first pre-emptive strike and claims the family's children will be handsomely rewarded, the result of judiciary expediency, bureaucratic insanity, empire building and an urgency to maintain the vast edifice of the welfare state.

Far too much intellectual and physical effort, resources and time is put into first creating the damage and then working on eradicating or alleviating the resulting effects, with very few resources going into actually resolving any of the underlying causal factors. While it is obviously important and necessary to alleviate the painful effects, those measures in themselves will do absolutely nothing to prevent the problems being repeated over and over again. Only the resolute tackling of the fundamental root causes will do that.

There have been many historic civil and human rights campaigns to right terrible wrongs inflicted by one dominant group of humans against another. In the end, however, there has always been a catalyst that triggered change, whether through violent revolution against intolerable conditions or quiet reform driven by the conscience of the silent majority.

At this point, we have no idea what that catalyst might be or who will provide such a trigger. However, as sure as night follows day, that change will eventually come. History tells us it always does. But who will initiate the debate and trigger the beginning of the end?

Could it perhaps be a new generation of politicians and lawmakers who want to right a historic wrong while scoring political leverage over their opponents? Might they, driven by some epiphany of conscience, or even just normal familial concern for their own children, suddenly realise the hypocrisy of the apologies delivered with such fervour by their forebears?

Could it be that with the changing demographic make-up of the community, one religious group will step forward and denounce the hegemony and the indiscriminate all-pervading bastardry and self-interest of institutions?

Could their conduct become such an anathema perhaps, that it can no longer be borne?

The Christian churches have been entirely gutless in the face of the secular destruction and denigration of traditional family life and important biological family kinship bonds. They have duly ignored the personal pain and dire outcomes for parents and their children, while clawing over each other in their rush for government handouts to provide support for the favoured victim group of the day.

The recent Royal Commission into institutional responses to child sexual abuse forced embattled religious institutions to stand by and watch community trust and respect ebb away. But perhaps their tarnish could be a blessing in disguise. Their atonement and redemption could yet turn out to come in a surprising form; especially since contrition and remorse today will earn them greater respect tomorrow.

For Christian churches, the landscape is actually changing and the opportunity to re-invigorate flagging support is a real possibility. They are no longer shackled to the skeletons of the past. This is particularly so since a mass of credible information has now come to light which confirms that the very government and non-governmental institutions that appropriately exposed the inexcusable cover-up of terrible institutional child abuse by religious institutions, are themselves actively engaged in covering up their own failings in the area of child and family protection.

This new information provides conclusive evidence that those who have been in the forefront of the condemnation of religious institutions for their failure to protect children, have themselves for the past 40 years failed their own duty of care obligations to prevent abuse and neglect. They have turned a blind eye to the pain and suffering their own policies and practices have inflicted on child victims and their powerless families.

Ironically, the realisation that religious institutions are now no longer shackled to the many skeletons in their closets is of vital importance. This means the disclosures, admissions and apologies for their failure to protect children in their care has set these institutions free to pursue a new path and introduce new initiatives, which could ultimately lead to the re-instatement of their once hallowed position as guardians of our moral compass.

It is hoped that our religious leadership is up to the task, and is able to recognise the challenges ahead and accept their responsibilities. They now have credible and necessary information available that allows them to question and challenge the policies and practices of their political, judicial and media critics. This would not only herald a new beginning in government/church relations, but also lead to the long overdue formulation and delivery of vastly improved child and family-protection policy outcomes, to which the community is unequivocally entitled.

But they will need to be able to communicate their message vigorously in the marketplace of ideas if they are to be successful in regaining their status.

Australian journalist Greg Sheridan pointed out the importance of the need for churches, the largest of which is the Catholic Church, to take a more proactive stand:

> Australia's Christian churches are in crisis, on the brink of complete strategic irrelevance. It's not clear they recognise the mortal depth of their problems. The churches need a new approach to their interaction with politics and the public debate, and to keeping themselves relevant in a post-Christian Australian society.[90]

But perhaps it will not actually be the Catholic Church at all that takes up such a challenge and lead the debate calling for urgent reforms. Or they may remain ignorant to a social justice problem that is busily engaged in destroying the lives of their congregations.

Historical precedents of leaders belonging to other Christian churches taking up the cause of important social justice issues can be found.

Take the case of William Wilberforce, an English politician, philanthropist and a leader of the movement to abolish the slave trade. A native of Kingston upon Hull in the north of England, he began his political career in 1780, eventually becoming the independent member of Parliament for Yorkshire. In 1785, he became an evangelical Christian, a move that resulted in major changes to his lifestyle and a lifelong concern for social reform. In 1787, he came into contact with Thomas Clarkson and a group of anti-slave-trade activists. They persuaded Wilberforce to take on the cause of abolition, and he soon

---

90 Sheridan, Greg. "Christian Churches Drifting Too Far from the Marketplace of Ideas." The Weekend Australian, 4 June 2016. Accessed here: www.theaustralian.com.au/opinion/columnists/greg-sheridan/christian-churches-drifting-too-far-from-the-marketplace-of-ideas/news-story/e641fab1f62b1a63b08cc1ec75634af5.

became one of the leading English abolitionists. He headed the parliamentary campaign against the British slave trade for 20 years until the passage of the Slave Trade Act 1807.

Such heroes are rare, however, and those willing to accept the difficult challenge of reforming contemporary family and child-protection legislation face an equally daunting task with little support and few rewards.

An embattled trade union movement is also searching for relevance in today's society. For them, a campaign to provide leadership for their members, many of whom are also targeted and beleaguered and have had their children removed from their protection, could prove extremely popular. To assume a leading role in a social justice campaign in support of better child-protection policies could be a win-win scenario and enhance its public image as a caring, family friendly force of good in our society. If the welfare of its membership is truly at the forefront of their concerns, then the desperate plight of its members' children should be of paramount interest to its leadership.

But time waits for no one, and perhaps it will be the Muslims who emphasise the great importance of marriage, family and children, and whose cultural customs and precepts diffuse disputation between couples and do not create vast welfare and bureaucratic edifices dedicated to the well-being of the single-parent family. Islam is a religion that promotes the importance of family as a central tenet of faith.

Could it be that policymakers will finally wake up to the disfiguring impact on their societies that low birth rates are having, a direct result of social policies that discourage, or at best fail, to encourage traditional family formation. The refugee crisis transfiguring the Western world's cultural and religious bases is driven in large part precisely by these low birth rates, and in a more enlightened age could be easily reversed.

Could change perhaps come following a possible enlightenment of the army of enabling social welfare professionals, who unwittingly continue to wreak so much havoc, mistakenly believing their actions to be in the *best interests* of those whose lives they are so busily destroying?

Could this transformation in thinking be wrought by a change in academia, in new works, texts and philosophies that will take a good long look at past practice and finally decide that change is necessary?

Could it come from the indigenous first nation people of the world, who have been the subject of such well-meaning national apologies but who have seen nothing in their own lives change? The lyrical apologies delivered by state and national governments in Australia to Aboriginal people whose children were removed by church and state authorities, the "Stolen Generations", may have exonerated the souls of Anglo-Saxons, but years on more children than ever are being removed from the protection of their families, with far too many of them ending up in institutional care. At the same time, more and more adults than ever are incarcerated for simply trying to remain in the lives of their children. The vain attempts to protect their biological offspring from harm vilified.

At the height of the American civil rights campaigns for recognition and equal rights in the late 60s and early 70s, Black Panther leader Fred Hampton, was, unexpectedly, able to enlist the support of some unlikely, but equally oppressed, minority groups, who agreed to join forces with the Panthers in their common objective of social-justice-for-all, civil-rights campaigns.

The time when child-protection advocates realise the full extent of large-scale child removals taking place across the whole of the community and become creative may not be that far away. Enlisting the support of equally persecuted and disenfranchised fellow citizens and creating a united front in support of child-protection changes is very likely to unfold in coming years. Unfortunately, for many children and their biological families it will be far too little, far too late.

Perhaps change could even come from an enlightened media organisation that wants to differentiate itself from its competitors. Periodic insight and progressive analyses of the present debacle have in the past withered on the vine. Despite the best efforts of a few courageous and campaigning journalists, nothing has changed the status quo. The present power structures have become even more entrenched in the face of criticism, and the intransigence of ideologically driven groups has become even more uncompromising.

But a new generation of emerging journalists, less ideologically hidebound than their forebears, might just be able to cast a clearer eye over what has been so obvious to so many for so long.

Perhaps it will ultimately be something as simple as the voices of the victims, the souls of those damaged by the present system, those who have seen the suffering of their parents and their siblings, their neighbours and workmates, who have themselves been damaged sufficiently to bear witness.

We might never know. But in some small way we hope that this book will be one small brick in the transformation to come.

* * *

In the End, we will remember not the words of our enemies, but the silence of our friends.

Martin Luther King, Jr.

Acknowledgements

THIS BOOK WOULD not have been possible without the dedication and support of numerous people, including Debbie Cook, whose commitment and understanding of the need to expose the system for what it is supported me all the way through the earlier stages of the development of the Family Briefing investigative team and the extended project. Convinced this was not a gender issue, her attitude was always: "We need to re-examine and better understand the missing links that are preventing us from learning the truth. Let's find out what lies behind the facade of the system."

Michael Riddell's cheery enthusiasm for the project during part of the concluding two years of research and analysis helped to drive the pursuit for answers. Bronwyn White has also been very supportive of the project, of which this book is only one small part, and I wish to thank them both for their much appreciated encouragement.

I would also like to thank Trevor Miller, a long-time friend and colleague, for his vital support. His extensive experience in TV production as a respected professional editor and producer as well as his deep understanding of the vagaries of "the system" has proven to be extremely important.

Most particularly, I would like to thank journalist, author and publisher John Stapleton, for his invaluable practical assistance in helping to bring this project to fruition. Without his expert media knowledge and guidance on storytelling, the exposure of this human tragedy may never have materialised.

Above all, I especially wish to thank my dear daughter Brooke, for her unwavering support and her mature and balanced approach throughout some extremely challenging times. Without her guiding sense of fairness, resilience and love for both of her parents equally throughout the whole of her formative childhood years, the writing of this book would never have transpired.

And most particularly, I would like to thank the unfailing support of Christine Ware. Without her, I may not have survived those frantic early years, of what would turn out to be a life-changing experience. The consistent support throughout my journey from many dear friends and family members, in particular Karen, Leah, Michael, Jessica, Kyle, Gabby, Bruce, Lindsay, Melanie, Alan, Brad, Ross, Marg, Lara, Rick, Liz, Tyson and Frieda, has proven invaluable and I thank them greatly for their balanced dependability. I would also like to acknowledge Jessica Bell for her lovely cover design. It is no wonder she has earned a reputation as one of the world's leading designers.

Fondly remembered for their dedication during those hectic years of radio production in support of beleaguered families, are Phillip York and Ian Purdie. Their untiring enthusiasm and reliability, was second to none. I especially wish to express my sincere gratitude to Greg Andresen for his enduring patience and valuable expert technical assistance. Of particular value was his practical guidance on the many difficulties faced when questioning and challenging the status quo in order to expose the myriad of inaccuracies in media reporting of family and child-protection matters.

To all the unsung heroes who blew the whistle from the inside and whose names we cannot mention, our sincere gratitude for your courage and conviction, as well as the risks you took, to get us over the line.

Since this book is able to provide a documented snapshot in time on how society manages the protection of its children, your collective efforts to bring this to the attention of an unsuspecting community will not be in vain.

About the Author

BORN IN HOLLAND, the eldest of five children, Peter van de Voorde migrated to Australia with his family where they spent the first four years living in a tent on the northern beaches of Sydney. Adventurous and with an early love of music, carpentry, horses and farming, he went on to become a musician and entertainer, licensed builder, farmer, resort manager and ultimately a researcher, producer and broadcaster. His entertainment career included writing and recording a top-10 hit single, TV appearances and a seven-month tour of Southeast Asia entertaining troops during the Vietnam War.

Eventually, Peter combined all his interests by first designing, building and then managing for 20 years a popular country holiday resort. But a life-changing event occurred that would have an impact on the rest of his life and cause him to commence a totally unexpected journey of discovery. Profoundly disturbed by what he found and shocked by the experiences of the people he met, the writing of this book became inevitable.

www.ingramcontent.com/pod-product-compliance
Lightning Source LLC
Chambersburg PA
CBHW071902290426
44110CB00013B/1244